WITHDRAWN

REAL PEOPLE WORKING *in*

SALES & MARKETING

REAL PEOPLE WORKING *in*

SALES & MARKETING

Blythe Camenson

Printed on recyclable paper

VGM Career Horizons
a division of *NTC Publishing Group*
Lincolnwood, Illinois USA

Library of Congress Cataloging-in-Publication Data
Camenson, Blythe.
   Real people working in sales and marketing / Blythe Camenson.
      p.   cm.—(On the job)
   Includes bibliographical references (p.).
   ISBN 0-8442-4728-6. (hc : alk. paper).—ISBN 0-8442-4729-4 (pbk. :
   alk. paper)
   1. Marketing—Vocational guidance. I. Title. II. Series.
HF5415.35.C36 1996
658.8'0023'73—dc20   96-28073
                                          CIP

Published by VGM Career Horizons, a division of NTC Publishing Group
4255 West Touhy Avenue
Lincolnwood (Chicago), Illinois 60646-1975, U.S.A.

67890 VL 987654321

Dedication

In memory of my grandmother, Bess Sachs

Contents

Acknowledgments

The author would like to thank the following professionals for providing information about their careers:

- Theresa Bulmer, Manager, Cabbages Health Emporium

- Vivian Portela Buscher, Travel Agent

- LeAnne Coury, Director of Sales, Quality Suites Hotel

- Chad Ellis, Account Executive, Kimberly-Clark

- Chris Fuller, Food Services General Manager, Thomas J. Lipton

- Beatrice Marti, Salesperson, Saks Fifth Avenue

- Al Mendoza, Proprietor, Keepsake Flowers and Gifts, Director, American International Academy of Floral Design

- Mary Fallon Miller, Travel Agent

- Colleen Newshott, Real Estate Broker, Newshott Realty

- Adam Perl, Antiques Dealer, Pastimes

- Mary Ptak, Co-owner, The Stock Exchange

- Pat Reese, Flower Broker, Floral International Xpress

- Bernice Ricciardelli, Insurance Agent, State Farm Insurance

- Jim Ridolfi, Auctioneer, Aspon Trading Company

- Ernie Stetenfeld, Public Relations Director, AAA Wisconsin

- Brent Van Ham, Cashier, J. D. Streett Mobil Service Station

- Kevin Whelan, Product Manager, Hill-Rom

About the Author

A full-time writer of career books, Blythe Camenson's main concern is helping job seekers make educated choices. She firmly believes that with enough information, readers can find long-term, satisfying careers. To that end, she researches traditional as well as unusual occupations, talking to a variety of professionals about what their jobs are really like. In all of her books she includes first-hand accounts from people who can reveal what to expect in each occupation, the upsides as well as the down.

Camenson's interests range from history and photography to writing novels. She is also director of Fiction Writer's Connection, a membership organization providing support to new and published writers.

Camenson was educated in Boston, earning her B.A. in English and psychology from the University of Massachusetts and her M.Ed. in counseling from Northeastern University.

In addition to *On the Job: Real People Working in Sales and Marketing*, the other books she has written for VGM Career Horizons are:

Career Portraits: Travel

Career Portraits: Writing

Career Portraits: Nursing

Career Portraits: Firefighting

Careers for History Buffs

Careers for Plant Lovers

Careers for Health Nuts

Careers for Mystery Buffs

Careers for Self-Starters

Great Jobs for Communications Majors

On the Job: Real People Working in Health and Medicine

On the Job: Real People Providing Services

Opportunities in Museums

Opportunities in Teaching English to Speakers of Other Languages

How to Use This Book

On the Job: Real People Working in Sales and Marketing is part of a series designed as companion books to the *Occupational Outlook Handbook*. The *OOH*, as it is commonly called, is a great reference book useful for librarians, guidance and career counselors, as well as job seekers. It provides information on hundreds of careers, focusing on the following subjects:

Nature of the Work

Working Conditions

Employment

Training, Other Qualifications, and Advancement

Job Outlook

Earnings

Related Occupations

Sources of Additional Information

What the *OOH* doesn't provide is a first-hand look at what any particular job is really like. And that's where our *On the Job* series picks up the slack. In addition to providing an overview of each field, training and education requirements, salary expectations, related fields, and sources to pursue for further information, *On the Job* authors have talked to dozens of professionals and experts in the various fields.

These first-hand accounts tell what each job really entails, what the duties are, what the lifestyle is like, what the upsides and downsides are. All of the professionals reveal what drew them to the field and how they got started. And so you can make the best career choice for yourself, each professional offers you some expert advice based on years of personal experience.

Each chapter also lets you see at a glance, with easy to reference symbols, the level of education and salary range required for the featured occupations.

So, how do you use this book? Easy. You don't need to run to the library or buy a copy of the *OOH*. All you have to do is glance through our extensive table of contents, find the fields that interest you, and read what the experts have to say.

Introduction to the Field

Billions of dollars are spent each year on all types of products and services. In such a consumer-oriented society, the need for sales and marketing professionals continues to grow.

If you're reading this book, chances are you're already considering a career in one of the many areas of this wide-open occupational category. Glancing through the table of contents will give you an idea of all the choices open to you.

But perhaps you're not sure of the working conditions the different fields offer or which area would suit your personality, skills, and lifestyle the most. There are several factors to consider when deciding which sector of sales and marketing to pursue. Each field carries with it different levels of responsibility and commitment. To identify occupations that will match your expectations, you need to know what each job entails.

Ask yourself the following questions and make note of your answers. Then, as you go through the following chapters, compare your requirements to the information provided by the professionals interviewed inside. Their comments will help you pinpoint the fields that would interest you, and eliminate those that would clearly be the wrong choice.

- How much of a people person are you? Do you prefer to work face to face with clients or customers, or are you more comfortable with telephone contact?

- Do you want a desk job, or would you prefer to be out and about, traveling and covering a wide territory? Some occupations offer more freedom of movement than others.

- How much time are you willing to commit to training? Some skills can be learned on-the-job or in a year or two of formal training; others can take considerably longer.

- How much money do you expect to earn starting out and after you have a few years' experience under your belt? Salaries and earnings vary greatly in each chosen sales and marketing profession. Some sales workers earn just the minimum wage, others work for salary plus commission and earn much more.

- How much independence do you require? Do you want to be your own boss or will you be content as a salaried employee?

- Will you work normal hours? Or will your day start at 5:30 A.M. and not end until 13 or 14 hours later? Can you handle working on holidays and weekends, or do you want that time free?

- How much stress can you handle? Would you prefer to avoid work that could be emotional draining?

Knowing what your expectations are, then comparing them to the realities of the work will help you make informed choices.

Although *On the Job: Real People Working in Sales and Marketing* strives to be as comprehensive as possible, not all jobs in this extensive field have been covered or given the same amount of emphasis. Several categories of sales and marketing professions have merited their own book. You will find information on other sales and marketing positions in the following *"On the Job"* books published by VGM Career Horizons:

> *On the Job: Real People Working in Service Businesses*
> *On the Job: Real People Working in Communications*

If you still have questions after reading this book, there are a number of other avenues to pursue. You can find out more information by contacting the sources listed at the end of each chapter. You can also find professionals on your own to talk to and observe as they go about their work. Any remaining gaps you discover can be filled by referring to the *Occupational Outlook Handbook*.

CHAPTER 1 Retail Sales

OVERVIEW

Millions of dollars are spent each day on all types of merchandise–everything from sweaters and cosmetics to lumber, office equipment, and plumbing supplies. Sales workers are employed by many types of retailers to assist customers in the selection and purchase of these items.

Whether selling antiques, computer equipment, or automobiles, a sales worker's primary job is to interest customers in the merchandise. This may be done by describing the product's features, demonstrating its use, or showing various models and colors.

For some jobs, particularly those selling expensive and complex items, special knowledge or skills are needed. For example, workers who sell personal computers must be able to explain to customers the features of various brands and models, the meaning of manufacturers' specifications, and the types of software that are available.

In addition to selling, most retail sales workers make out sales checks; receive cash, check, and charge payments; bag or package purchases; and give change and receipts. Depending on the hours they work, they may have to open or close the cash register. This may include counting the money in the cash register; separating charge slips, coupons, and exchange vouchers; and making deposits at the cash office. Sales workers are often held responsible for the contents of their register, and repeated shortages are cause for dismissal in many organizations. (Cashiers, who have similar job duties, are discussed in Chapter 10.)

Sales workers can also handle returns and exchanges of merchandise, perform gift wrapping services, and keep their work areas neat. In addition, they may help stock shelves or racks, arrange for mailing or delivery of a purchase, mark price tags, take inventory, and prepare displays.

Sales workers must be aware of not only the promotions their store is sponsoring, but also those that are being sponsored by competitors. Also, they often must recognize possible security risks and know how to handle such situations.

Consumers often form their impressions of a store by its sales force. The retail industry is very competitive and, increasingly, employers are stressing the importance of providing courteous and efficient service. When a customer wants an item that is not on the sales floor, for example, the sales worker may check the stockroom and, if there are none there, place a special order or call another store to locate the item.

To provide better customer service, some firms employ personal shoppers. Some personal shoppers assist consumers in purchasing a particular item. For example, personal shoppers employed in department stores can assist customers in updating their wardrobes. Others actually choose the item for the client based on information provided. Those personal shoppers who work in food stores may buy groceries and arrange for their delivery to the customer's home.

Although most sales workers have many duties and responsibilities, in jobs selling standardized articles such as food, hardware, linens, and housewares, they often do little more than take payments and wrap purchases.

Many retail sales workers, however, need an extensive knowledge of the products they sell.

TRAINING

There usually are no formal education requirements for this type of work. Employers look for persons who enjoy working with people and have the tact and patience to deal with difficult customers. Among other desirable characteristics are an interest in sales work, a neat appearance, and the ability to communicate clearly and effectively. Before hiring, some employers may conduct a background check, especially for jobs in selling high-priced items.

In most small stores, an experienced employee or the proprietor instructs newly hired sales personnel in making out sales checks and operating the cash register. In larger stores, training programs are more formal and usually are conducted over several days.

Topics usually discussed are customer service, security, the store's policies and procedures, and how to work the cash register. Depending on the type of product they are selling, sales personnel may be given additional specialized training. For example, those working in cosmetics receive instruction on the types of products available and for whom they would be most beneficial. This training is often provided by a manufacturer's representative.

As salespersons gain experience and seniority, they usually move to positions of greater responsibility and are given their choice of departments. This often means moving to areas with potentially higher earnings and commissions. The highest earnings potential is usually found in selling big-ticket items. This work often requires the most knowledge of the product and the greatest talent for persuasion.

Traditionally, capable sales workers without a college degree could advance to management positions, but today, large retail businesses generally prefer to hire college graduates as management trainees, making a college education increasingly important. Despite this trend, capable employees without a college degree should still be able to advance to administrative or supervisory work in large stores.

Opportunities for advancement vary in small stores. In some establishments, advancement opportunities are limited because one person, often the owner, does most of the managerial work. In others, however, some sales workers are promoted to assistant managers.

Retail selling experience may be an asset when applying for sales positions with larger retailers or in other industries, such as financial services, wholesale trade, or manufacturing.

JOB OUTLOOK

Employment of retail sales workers is expected to increase about as fast as the average for all workers through the year 2005 due to anticipated growth in retail sales. In addition, numerous job openings will be created as sales workers transfer to other occupations or leave the labor force. As in the past, replacement needs will generate an exceptionally large number of sales jobs because the occupation is large and turnover is much higher than average. There will continue to be many opportunities for part-time workers, and demand will be strong for temporary workers during peak selling periods such as the Christmas season.

During recessions, sales volume and the resulting demand for sales workers generally decline. Purchases of costly items such as cars, appliances, and furniture tend to be postponed during difficult economic times. In areas of high unemployment, sales of all types of goods may decline. However, since turnover of sales workers is usually very high, employers often can control employment simply by not replacing all those who leave.

In some geographic areas, employers face a shortage of qualified applicants. As a result, employers can be expected to improve efforts to attract and retain workers by offering higher wages, more generous benefits, and more flexible schedules.

SALARIES

The starting salary for many part-time retail sales positions is the federal minimum wage. In some areas where employers are having difficulty attracting and retaining workers, wages are much higher than the established minimum.

The following list shows average weekly earnings by class of sales worker in several industries.

Motor vehicle and boats–$479

Radio, television, hi-fi, and appliances–$415

Furniture and home furnishings–$354

Hardware and building supplies–$323

Parts–$319

Other commodities–$269

Apparel–$255

Compensation systems vary by type of establishment and merchandise sold. Some sales workers receive an hourly wage. Others receive a commission or a combination of wages and commissions. Under a commission system, salespersons receive a percentage of the sales they make. These systems offer sales workers the opportunity to increase significantly their earnings, but they may find their earnings depend on their ability to sell their product and the ups and downs in the economy.

Benefits may be limited in smaller stores, but in large establishments they are usually comparable to those offered by other employers. In addition, nearly all sales workers are able to buy their store's merchandise at a discount, often from 10 to 40 percent below regular prices. In some cases, this privilege is extended to the employee's family as well.

RELATED FIELDS

Sales workers use sales techniques coupled with their knowledge of merchandise to assist customers and encourage purchases. These skills are used by people in a number of other occupations, including manufacturers' and wholesale trade sales workers, service sales representatives, counter and rental clerks, real estate sales agents, wholesale and retail buyers, insurance sales workers, and cashiers. All of these occupations are discussed throughout this book.

INTERVIEW

Beatrice Marti
Department Store Salesperson

Beatrice Marti started in 1993 working for Lord & Taylor, then in 1995 moved to Saks Fifth Avenue at the Town Centre Mall in Boca Raton, Florida.

 **EDUCATION**
H.S. Required

$$$ SALARY/EARNINGS
$12,000 to $20,000

What the Job's Really Like

"Right now I'm in the handbags department. For me, it's something new, I never thought much about buying handbags. Shoes, yes, dresses, yes, but I never knew that people bought so many handbags. It's unbelievable. Whenever there's a new style, the regular customers come hurrying in. In fact, we're the busiest department in the whole store.

"I deal mainly with the customers, trying to help them pick out a bag that they'll be happy with. Some are looking for quality and they don't care about the price; others have a certain budget to work with. Our bags range from $70 to more than $3,000. We even have one in stock now that costs $5,000. Most of our customers are very wealthy.

"My main concern is to make sure the customer leaves with a handbag that they are 100 percent happy about. If they're not happy I know that bag will end up being returned. And if it comes back to the store, then I don't make my quota. If I sense that they're not sure about a bag, I try to show them more merchandise so they can make a choice.

"Sometimes we get nasty customers and that can be difficult. You just try to ignore their behavior and deal with them cordially. I ring up the sales, put the purchases in shopping bags. I also have to keep the floor neat and make sure my counter is kept clean and that the handbags are kept in order.

"Not everyone does, but I think, as a salesperson, it's important that I dress well to come to work. When I go shopping myself, I have more confidence in someone who is dressed well. I feel they'll be able to give me better advice.

"I'm on my feet all day with this job. It was difficult when I first started, but you do get used to it. We get an hour for lunch and one twenty-minute break during the day. When we're busy, though, I don't bother with a break. It's more important to me to be on the floor selling. The time goes by very fast.

"I work any of the seven days, including holidays. But on Sundays and holidays I get paid time and a half. I get a paycheck each week, but it's calculated on an hourly basis, so if I miss a day of work, the hours are deducted.

"My hourly wage is $9 an hour, but it's figured in conjunction with a commission. There's a sales quota or goal we're expected to reach during each period and if we reach that goal, then we start receiving a commission. The goal is determined by your hourly wage. The lower your hourly wage, the lower the goal is and the easier it is to start making a commission. I wouldn't want to make any more than $9 an hour because then my goal would be higher and would take longer to reach.

"This is a new program that Saks just started a few months ago. Here's an example of what I'm talking about. The quota from August to January is $166,320. And it's divided up monthly. For example, for the month of September my goal was $19,958. In December, because of the Christmas holidays, my goal was $53,222. Sales were slow this year and I just made my goal on December 27. That left only four days to make a commission for that month. The commission is calculated at 5 percent of the gross sales after the goal is reached. I've earned a commission of $1,000 for the last five months. It's not really a lot of money–you can make much higher commissions in sales work outside of department stores. But the system does give you some incentives to work hard.

"I'm very happy at Saks; it's one of the best stores to work for. I have experience with only one other store, but I hear from other salespeople who've been in different situations and they all agree that Saks is the best. They treat you very well, like a person, not just like a selling machine. For example, on Saturdays and during the month of December they set out a lovely breakfast for all the personnel. And the management comes to the floor to help us when we're busy, even the general manager. They even give us presents.

"Of course, another of the benefits is that we get a very good discount on merchandise we want to buy. Thirty to forty percent. But I'm very careful not to spend my paycheck on things I don't need. We also have a good health plan and we get two weeks vacation a year and sick leave, too.

"Basically, it's a great job for me. I love selling and being around the merchandise. If I'm able to sell a handbag to someone who came into the store and hadn't really planned on buying one, then it makes me feel good. It's very satisfying."

How Beatrice Marti Got Started

"I'm from Colombia and this is the first time I worked in the States. I liked the hours I could work in a department store; some days I'll start late and that leaves me mornings to be at home and take care of the house and some days I finish early so I can be at home with the children. The hours are very flexible, but at the same time, the hours rotate so I never know too far ahead when I'm going to be off.

"I also liked the idea of working with fashion. When I was at Lord & Taylor's I worked with dresses and I liked that very much."

"I had no prior sales experience, just my high school diploma from Colombia, but I received on-the-job training. Some department stores will take you on with no experience, but others, such as Saks, won't. So after I was at Lord & Taylor's for a while, I then had enough experience to be hired at Saks."

Expert Advice

"If you want to work at Saks, I suggest you work at other stores first to get the experience you'll need. That's the way I did it.

"And of course, you have to enjoy working with people."

INTERVIEW

Adam Perl
Antiques Dealer

Adam Perl is the proprietor of Pastimes, an antiques and collectibles shop in Ithaca, New York.

What the Job's Really Like

"I specialize in about five or six areas I happen to have a particular love and feeling for–antique buttons, costume jewelry from the Victorian era through the forties, 1910 postcards, fountain pens, sterling silver, and antique beads. We also carry some oak furniture, glassware, and photographica. Pastimes is relatively small, but it looks like a well-organized and cleaned up flea market.

"You have to be careful about where you buy your merchandise. It's vital to make sure the auctioneers and dealers are reputable. There's a great deal of dishonesty in the business. A dealer might misrepresent an item's condition or authenticity. It's easy to get caught. Fairly recently a local dealer of questionable repute came across a big stash of mint-condition German lithographs that were reported to be from the turn of the century. We'd never seen anything like it–there are certain processes you just can't duplicate and this was one of them. The dealers were scarfing them up for $7 to $10 a piece. We found out they were repros, but not before a lot of us got stung.

"And 10 years ago I was selling some red-colored Fiestaware, a very popular deco dinnerware made by Homer Laughlin in the thirties, forties, and fifties. It turned out to be radioactive. Some of the glazes had been made with uranium.

"I love what I'm doing, always chasing after the next bargain, enjoying the wonderful thrill of the hunt, that feeling you get looking for treasures and bargains. It keeps you excited and fueled up when you're unloading your van in the cold rain, or you're stuck in the mud at an auction."

How Adam Perl Got Started

"If you scratch a dealer, you'll find a collector underneath. Many of us have gone into business just to finance our collecting habits. My own collecting habit began in the seventh grade when a classmate brought a book to school called *Cash for Your Coins*.

"But even if that hadn't happened, it's unlikely the collecting bug would have passed me by. I grew up surrounded by art and antiques; my mother is an art historian who worked at the Museum of Modern Art in New York, the Andrew Dickson White Museum at Cornell, and at the Smithsonian's Hirshhorn Museum. My father was a writer and both were serious antique collectors.

"I had never been to an auction until I was a young adult. I had just rented an unfurnished apartment when I found out about a country auction being held nearby.

"I was instantly hooked. I spent $100 and filled my van three times. I furnished my entire apartment with items left over to spare. The early seventies was a golden age of buying, when wonderful three- and four-generation estates were being broken up all over the country, but especially in the Northeast. There wasn't much of an antique market in any field then–you could buy anything for the proverbial song in those days.

"With no thought of turning it into a business at that time, I began frequenting auctions for the fun of it. I'd go out with $5 or $10 in my pocket and come home with treasures. I kept doing it over and over again, until I felt I had much more than I could fit in my apartment. I realized from seeing people's set-ups at flea markets that they had a organized system of pricing and that they generally specialized in a particular area, such as knives or dolls. I learned that if I took the things I bought and cleaned them up a bit–polished the brass, refinished the wood, and stove-blacked the iron–that I could actually sell them for more than I had paid for them. I had my first garage sale and made a little money on it. It wasn't much of a step from that to connect up with New York City and the contacts I had there.

"I talked to several dealers and tried to feel out people who were sympathetic and who would teach me. At the time the world of antiques was pretty much a mystery; there was this arcane underground where people wouldn't reveal their secrets or knowledge to anyone.

"I found sympathetic antique dealers at American Hurrah, which is now a well-known shop run by Joel and Kate Kopp, specializing in quilts and photographic images. The Kopps were very forthcoming and didn't hold anything back. They taught me you try to double your money. You don't always do it, or sometimes you do better, but that's what you aim for. They taught me how to judge the condition of an item, and how to develop and trust your own taste. They also helped to bail me out when I made mistakes.

"I became a "picker", a term in the industry for a wholesaler. The picker, during his antique hunting expeditions, tries to pick out the one great item out of the 10,000 he sees. I would actually buy retail at shops in upstate New York, perhaps finding a quilt, beautifully made and in excellent condition, for $25 to $50. I would take them to the city and sell them for double.

"The Kopps had taught me to look for the fine cotton quilts that were hand-stitched with good colors and good patterns and early nineteenth-century materials. I had bought a quilt at a garage sale for $4 but it didn't meet any of that criteria. It was thick, heavy wool, twentieth-century, rather ugly. But still, there was something about it that was really striking. It had a man's wool tanktop bathing suit stitched into it, complete with its Sears Roebuck label. I took this to New York, but the Kopps didn't think much of it. But they were always very nice to me; they bought the quilt for $12 and I was relieved. Later they turned around and were able to sell it for $50. This quilt was sold many times, and eventually ended up in the Louvre Museum in Paris, as an important example of early twentieth-century American folk art. Anybody who's been in business has made mistakes from time to time. Incidents like this can happen to the best of us.

"I opened my first shop in 1973 with just $400. A condemned high school had just been bought by an architect who remodeled it and converted it into a lively arcade of shops and boutiques called the DeWitt Building. I rented an unpretentious hole-in-the-wall for $125 a month plus one month's security. The landlord gave me some paint and I bought a huge old machine-made oriental rug for one dollar. The rug had several feet missing in the corner. I spent another dollar and bought a big over-stuffed chair to cover the hole. After the two dollars I spent on decor, I had $148 left for merchandise.

"I left the business for a few years, then returned in 1978 to open my current shop, Pastimes. This is one of the best businesses to get into on little or no capital. You don't need any particular expertise, or any particular degree. You do need to have some stock and a couple of tables and table coverings. And then you can hit the flea markets. You can still find perfectly good flea markets where you can set up for $10 to $25. Later you can graduate to a little bit higher caliber show, whose fees might be from $35 to $100. A lot of people just do shows. It's the exception actually having a retail shop. You're tied down and have the overhead.

"Many people get started in this business as they're heading toward retirement. They ease into it the last 5 or 10 years of their working career, and then do it as a retirement business to supplement their pensions and social security income.

"And, it's a recession-resistant business. When times are hard, antiques are a better buy than new items. People are shopping more carefully and even non-collectors who just want to get good practical furniture, tools, or gifts will turn to antiques."

Expert Advice

"There are probably more than 10,000 branches in the antiques and collectibles business. Some collectors specialize in nothing but actual items used in the Civil War. You can take any particular area of your interest, whether it be local history, silver making, the history of advertising, woodworking, tools, lace making, or photographica, and turn that one area into a whole specialty and a whole business.

"Look for an area you love and learn more about it and concentrate in it.

"I am also a firm believer that in this business the less money you have the better. I knew a young man who had inherited $50,000. This was many years ago when that was really a lot of money. He went out and bought every exquisite piece of furniture he could find. I remember at the auctions I was very jealous; he could outbid everybody. He opened up a shop with all those beautiful things, but he couldn't sell them because he'd paid too much for them. You have to develop through experience knowledge of what the market will bear. There's no substitute for the actual buying and selling of merchandise to learn about the market and pricing. There are thousands of antique price guides, but this is something you can't really learn by the book. It's best to get into it gradually, go to a lot of antique shows and shops, compare prices, do your homework.

INTERVIEW

Jim Ridolfi
Auctioneer

Jim Ridolfi is the owner of the Aspon Trading Company in Troy, Pennsylvania. He has been an auctioneer since 1992.

What the Job's Really Like

"First you need a chant, and everyone develops their own. I try not to use too many words–the people won't understand you. What they're listening for is the numbers. You learn a basic method at auctioneer training school, and then you take it and refine it and make it into your own.

"I advertise my services in newspapers and have made contacts with other antique dealers, estate attorneys, and will executors.

"Auctioneers hold their events indoors in hotel ballrooms or outside in a farmer's field or an estate's back yard. We work on a percentage basis earning between 15 and 30 percent of the price of each item sold. We handle anything from antiques and collectibles to household items, livestock, and real estate."

How Jim Ridolfi Got Started

"Attending auctions started off as a hobby, but then I realized I enjoyed it even more than my previous occupation–I was an environmental engineer. I decided to pursue it as a profession. Like me, many auctioneers are also antique dealers. Although I don't do much of that now–it's pretty much straight auctioning these days–I specialized in old phonographs and radios and I have a particular love for mid- to late-nineteenth century items. From selling my own inventory, it was an easy leap to selling inventory for others.

"I went through a training program before I hung out my shingle. Because I'm in Pennsylvania it was required that I attend the state-sponsored auctioneering school. The program is held at the Harrisburg Area Community College and runs for 15 straight weekends, eight hours a day on both Saturday and Sunday.

"It was presented as a series of six mini-courses. One was on developing your chant; another covered pre-auction activities such as advertising, appraising, and procurement; the third course covered the mechanics of running an auction; then post-auction activities such as making payment to clients and following up; and the sixth component covered business and accounting skills."

Expert Advice

"It's important to get good training. Training programs can run from two weeks to three or four months, depending on your state's requirements. While in training, auctioneers also study communications skills, the law as applied to auctioneers, marketing, auction management, appraisal, and selling real estate.

"Different states have different licensing laws. Some states have none at all, some are very rigorous with what they require.

"Many auctioneers go through various national auctioneering schools; the best known one is the Missouri Auction School. But it's important to check first which schools your state will accept. Pennsylvania, for example, only accepts training through the two schools in Pennsylvania. The best thing to do is contact your state licensing board and find out what they require, then write or call The National Auctioneers Association (their address is listed at the end of this chapter) to find out about their training."

INTERVIEW

Mary Ptak
Vintage Clothing Sales

Mary Ptak is co-owner of the Stock Exchange, a vintage clothing shop in Fort Lauderdale, Florida. Mary and her partner, Carol Levin, have been in business since 1986.

What the Job's Really Like

"The Stock Exchange carries clothes ranging in price from $5 for an Indian cotton gauze blouse from the sixties to a $2000 Schaparelli gown. We also handle rentals, outfit murder mysteries, and have supplied the costumes for several major television shows and motion pictures, including *Key West, Cape Fear,* and *Wrestling Ernest Hemingway.*

"I travel all over the country to look for just the right pieces. I also have built up a network of people who ship me good finds.

"Over the years we've managed to build up an international clientele, including collectors from Japan, Germany, and England. Our customers are an eclectic mix of people. People from England and Japan have been buying up everything they can find from the fifties. Our serious collectors tend to buy clothes from the thirties through the fifties–Joan Crawford, Great Gatsby, and Garbo styles with big padded shoulders and lots of sparkly glitz. Lilli Ann suits from the forties and fifties are popular now, too. They're extremely classy looking, nipped in at the waist with flaring peplums. Some of our customers are Victorian period collectors; but most people now want the article they're buying to be useful–they want to be able to wear it. Local kids are demanding sixties and seventies garments. The kids even want the polyester nik-nik shirts from the sixties–foul-looking things, but they're popular now. The kids are always a little more savvy than the general public and they start fashion trends with their regular street clothes. I used to be able to buy what I liked, now I have to think in terms of my customers' needs.

"I learned what was collectible from being in the business a long time. You have to have a good eye to pick what people want and you have to change with the times–trends are constantly changing and you can't always be buying the same things."

How Mary Ptak Got Started

"I wanted to spend all my time in people's attics. I was mainly interested in finding old-style clothing. When I was in college in the sixties, I would just literally knock on strangers' doors and ask them if I could clean out their attics. In those days, they were usually delighted for you to do that.

"But times have changed, and people are much more aware of the treasures they might have stored away. Gone are the days when you could pick up something for 25 cents or under.

"Carol and I were both dissatisfied with our jobs, and one day we just decided to take the plunge. Carol loves the sales end of the business, dealing with the customers, and I satisfy my shopping urges by traveling around the country as the Stock Exchange's buyer.

"The Stock Exchange is a classic example of laughing all the way to the bank. In 1986 no one would give us a business loan. They didn't think we'd make it."

Expert Advice

"For anyone considering a similar business, it's important to buy clothes that are in excellent condition, unless it's something that's really ancient and people would expect there to be damage. And you also need a huge amount of stock. When we started out we had very little, but we took consignments then, and because I'm a fanatic shopper, it didn't take long to build it up.

"We've also managed to build ourselves a first class reputation. We make an effort to pay people what they deserve for their merchandise—it's one of the reasons we've been so successful."

INTERVIEW

Theresa Bulmer
Retail Food Sales

Theresa Bulmer is manager of Cabbages Health Emporium, a natural food store. Natural food stores are specialty shops selling a wide range of healthful foods and related items such as vitamins and food supplements. Employees in natural food stores must be knowledgeable about the different foods and products and be able to answer a wide range of customer questions.

Cabbages Health Emporium opened its doors in 1991 as a market stocking health-oriented products. They offer a line of organic produce, organic foods, and nonorganic frozen foods and groceries. They avoid food with preservatives, refined sugars, or additives. They will not sell any food that has been irradiated to prolong its shelf life.

What the Job's Really Like

"Cabbages Health Emporium customers are people with special diet or health needs, and those who just live a natural, healthy lifestyle, including vegans and vegetarians. We have a cafe and a vegan deli and we also cater to sports enthusiasts and body builders, stocking several lines of sports drinks and powders and different types of vitamins and formulas. In addition, we carry a line of environmentally safe cleaning products that are biodegradable with no harsh chemicals.

"The duties of a manager vary from store to store. I do a little of everything. I do ordering, I take out garbage, clean bathrooms, ring up sales, work on store operating policies, talk to brokers, sales reps, and distributors, six days a week from 7:30 in the morning to 6:00 at night. I also supervise ten employees.

"And I talk to customers and try to keep them happy. The customers are wonderful, really. They can learn from us and we can learn from them. Someone will come in with a product I've never seen before. I'll ask what you take it for and they'll rattle off everything the product can do and I get really excited because I'm learning something new.

"Some of our customers are real knowledgeable, sometimes even more knowledgeable than we are, and then we have those who are clueless. They tell us it's their first time in a health food store and they don't know what they should be buying. We're all customer-service oriented here, and if anyone is unable to help a customer we refer him to someone else.

"I really like this store and I enjoy what I do. But being a store manager, even in a health food store, can lend itself to stress. You have employees underneath you, an owner above you, customers, all kinds of salespeople, and you're being pulled in a lot of different directions. You need a lot of patience, a lot of love.

"The health food business doesn't pay very well, but you don't do it for the money. You're in the health food business to be in the health food business.

"Entry-level salaries usually are quite low, from $5 to $6 an hour, depending on your knowledge and skills and the area of the country in which you work. As you climb up the ladder, the pay scale doesn't necessarily climb with you.

"To me this is a way of life. The more people who know about organic food and health, the healthier we will be as a society on a whole. The more farmers who grow organic and the more people who buy organic, the sooner prices will go down and products will be more readily available. Then more people can be turned on to this way of life.

"I know people who have gone from doctors and pills and medication and have changed their lifestyle and now no longer need the doctors and pills and medication. I'm not downgrading traditional medicine; there are many people who have been helped that way. But there are alternatives and if we begin to look at them and if the holistic professionals and the doctors begin to work with each other as opposed to against each other, we can change lives."

How Theresa Got Started

"I've been into a more healthy lifestyle for a lot of years, but I had no idea I'd end up in a health food store and really like it. I was unemployed back in 1990 and knowing very little about health food stores or the health food industry itself, I walked into a place that was being built. I got the job that same day, and now I'm the manager. Ever since the first day, I've been led in this direction.

"I had a sales background and some skills but very little training, so I learned on the job. You'll find that a lot of people learn on the job in the health food industry. Unless you're going to school to learn about health and nutrition, you end up being self-taught."

Expert Advice

"It's been my experience that many health food stores are very open to training new employees. At Cabbages we look for certain qualities in job candidates. We want to see a good attitude, a strong interest, and willingness to learn. It's usually obvious when you interview someone, when you talk to them.

"My advice, in addition to scanning help wanted ads, job seekers should stop by the stores where they would like to work. At Cabbages we don't advertise when we have an opening. We would put a sign in the window or check around through word of mouth."

(For more information about food services, see Chapter 5.)

● ● ●

INTERVIEW
Al Mendoza
Retail Florist

Al Mendoza is proprietor of Keepsake Flowers and Gifts in Dolton, Illinois.

He is also director of the American International Academy of Floral Design.

What the Job's Really Like

"Florists either own and operate their own shops or work in a shop for someone else. There are three kinds of flower shops: cash and carry stores, decorator shops, and service shops.

"Cash and carry stores, or merchandising stores as they are also known, sell bunches of pre-wrapped flowers. Generally, customers cannot order special arrangements through cash and carry shops; their selections are limited to what is immediately available and on-hand. Cash and carry shops are found in the neighborhood supermarket's flower section, at farmers' markets, or at impromptu "shops" set up in buckets alongside of the road.

"Decorator shops, which are few and far between, operate as specialists, custom-making arrangements for important occasions such as weddings or balls. They generally do not cater to walk-in customers.

"The largest percentage of florists are service florists, meaning they offer a service in addition to a product. They design and custom-make and deliver their merchandise.

"The jobs available in florist shops include: owner, manager, salesperson, floral designer, delivery personnel, interiorscaping and maintenance personnel.

"Florists work long hours and when most people are out enjoying the various parties, you're working at them. During holiday times, most people are having fun, enjoying the festivities, but again, it's the busiest time of the year for florists. In the floral world you don't get weekends and holidays off. I can't remember the last time my family and I could share a decent holiday together. Christmas, Easter. You're working like crazy the week before, then you're so exhausted, you can't enjoy yourself.

"Although salaries vary in different parts of the country, entry-level floral designers with little or no experience can expect to earn minimum wage to five or six dollars an hour. In the flower business you're paid according to productivity and your design ability. Someone who is a good, fast, productive designer can make more money. It can go up to eight, nine, or ten dollars an hour. Then when you move up into management positions, your salary goes up from there. Your pay scale is not based on how much schooling you've had or how much you know, but how much and how well you actually do.

"To start a florist shop these days an initial investment of about $50,000 would be required. And in today's economy, you can expect to work eight to ten years before realizing a profit.

"It's a risk when you're dealing with perishables. A person could lose a lot if they don't know how to order. If they order too much they can lose, or if they don't order enough they can lose. A typical example would be Valentine's Day. If you order too many roses, if you buy a thousand too many, you can lose thousands of dollars. But it's hard to learn how to get the ordering right. That's why it's so important to work for other florists before venturing out on your own. You need the experience.

"Many floral designers get their training working in a florist shop, learning as they go. They also attend seminars and workshops and take courses at floral design schools.

"At the American International Academy of Floral Design students study art and mechanics. The art is what you see in a design, the mechanics are how you put it together. As a teacher, I stress more the mechanics than the art. The art will come to them naturally, the colors and the choice of flowers and the mixing, but the basic foundations of design are more important, what it is you need to make this whole composition come together.

"For further training, students attend seminars and workshops sponsored by local wholesalers or the AIFD, the American Institute of Floral Design, which is the professional association to which floral designers strive to belong. But admission to this organization is very competitive.

"A three-week course is enough to help a student get his foot in the door at a flower shop. But really, three weeks is not enough. The rest of the training comes from on-the-job experience. But it's a Catch-22 situation. It's difficult to get that first job without some sort of training. Our program helps to open the door."

How Al Mendoza Got Started

"I got involved when I was a young person, about 14. There was a florist shop along my paper route and they were looking for a stock boy. I worked my way up to delivery, then apprentice florist. I also studied in Europe and at the American Art Floral School. Eventually, I started teaching there and I was assistant director. I was with them from 1980 through 1995, then I opened my own school, the American International Academy of Floral Design.

"I always enjoyed working with flowers. I find the art to be exciting, different. It's an excellent medium to work with."

Expert Advice

"I always tell any student who is coming to our school and planning on opening up a flower shop that it's great to know floral design, but it's more important to have a business degree than a floral degree. More businesses fail because they think of it as an art business rather than an actual commercial business. If someone wants to get their training through college, they should major in business with a minor in floral design.

"As with any business that hopes to garner off-the-street customers, location is always the first consideration. Because flowers are considered to be more a luxury item than a necessity, most successful florist shops are found in suburban town centers as opposed to downtown, inner city locations. Florist shops also can do well in shopping malls.

"To be a successful florist, a love of plants, although crucial, is not enough. Florists must have training in every aspect of the industry, including strong business skills. The best preparation is gaining a combination of on-the-job experience and education.

"Trainees can gain experience working part-time for retail and wholesale florists, for greenhouses and nurseries, or for cut flower growers. With this kind of exposure, potential florists can learn about packing and unpacking, processing, shipping, propagation, cutting, seed sowing, bulb planting and potting, the basics of floral design, and pickup, delivery, and sales work.

"While in school, students should take courses in biological sciences, math, communications, computer science, and general business, including retail store management.

"Some academic and vocational institutions offer two- and four-year programs geared directly to floriculture and horticulture. Many also provide students with the opportunity for training while in school through cooperative education programs. Coop programs place students in related business settings and, after the first year of academics, alternate semesters with work and study.

"The Society of American Florists has prepared a list of colleges, universities, and post-secondary schools offering two- and four-year degree programs and technical and certificate-awarding programs. The courses cover general horticulture, ornamental horticulture, floriculture, and floral design." (The Society's address can be found at the end of this chapter.)

● ● ●

FOR MORE INFORMATION

Information on careers in retail sales may be obtained from the personnel offices of local stores; from state merchants' associations; or from local unions of the United Food and Commercial Workers International Union.

In addition, general information about retailing is available from:

National Retail Federation
701 Pennsylvania Avenue, N.W.
Washington, DC 20004-2608

To find out about training programs for auctioneers, write to:

The National Auctioneers Association
8880 Ballentine
Overland Park, KS 66214

For more information about the floral industry, contact:

American Floral Art School
529 South Wabash Ave, #600
Chicago, Ill 60605-1679

American Floral Services
P.O. Box 12309
Oklahoma City, OK 73157

American Florists Association
2525 Heathcliff
Reston, VA 22091

American Institute of Floral Designers
720 Light Street
Baltimore, MD 21230-3816

American International Academy of Floral Design
8 South Michigan Ave, Suite 210
Chicago, IL 60603

Society of American Florists
1601 Duke Street
Alexandria, VA 22314-3406

CHAPTER 2 Services Sales Representatives

EDUCATION
B.A. Recommended

$$$ SALARY/EARNINGS
$20,000 to $40,000

OVERVIEW

Services sales representatives sell a wide variety of services. For example, sales representatives for data processing services firms sell complex services such as inventory control, payroll processing, sales analysis, and financial reporting systems.

Hotel sales representatives contact government, business, and social groups to solicit convention and conference business for the hotel.

Fundraisers plan programs to raise money for charities or other nonprofit causes. Sales representatives for temporary help services firms locate and acquire clients who will hire the firm's employees.

Telephone services sales representatives visit commercial customers to review their telephone systems, analyze their communications needs, and recommend services such as installation of additional equipment. Other representatives sell automotive leasing, public utility, burial, shipping, protective, and management consulting services.

Services sales representatives act as industry experts, consultants, and problem solvers when selling their firm's services. The sales representative, in some cases, creates demand for his or her firm's services. A prospective client who is asked to consider buying a particular service may never have used, or even been aware of a need for, that service. For example, wholesalers might be persuaded to order a list of credit ratings for checking their customers' credit prior to making sales, and discover that the list could be used to solicit new business.

There are several different categories of services sales jobs:

OUTSIDE SALES REPRESENTATIVES call on clients and prospects at their homes or offices. They may have an appointment, or they may practice cold calls, arriving without an appointment.

INSIDE SALES REPRESENTATIVES work on their employer's premises, assisting individuals interested in the company's services.

TELEMARKETING SALES REPRESENTATIVES sell exclusively over the telephone. They make large numbers of calls to prospects, attempting to sell the company's service themselves, or to arrange an appointment between the prospect and an outside sales representative. Some sales representatives deal exclusively with one, or a few, major clients.

Despite the diversity of services being sold, the jobs of all services sales representatives have much in common. All sales representatives must fully understand and be able to discuss the services their company offers.

Also, the procedures they follow are similar. Many sales representatives develop lists of prospective clients through telephone and business directories, asking business associates and customers for leads, and calling on new businesses as they cover their assigned territory. Some services sales representatives acquire clients through inquiries about their company's services.

Regardless of how they first meet the client, all services sales representatives must explain how the services being offered can meet the client's needs. This often involves demonstrations of their company's services. They answer questions about the nature and cost of the services and try to overcome objections in order to persuade potential customers to purchase the services. If they fail to make a sale on the first visit, they may follow up with more visits, letters, or phone calls. After closing a sale, services sales representatives generally follow up to see that the purchase meets the customer's needs, and to determine if additional services can be sold.

Because services sales representatives obtain many of their new accounts through referrals, their success hinges on developing a satisfied clientele who will continue to use the services and will recommend them to other potential customers. Like other types of sales jobs, a services sales representative's reputation is crucial to his or her success.

Services sales work varies with the kind of service sold. Selling highly technical services, such as communications systems or computer consulting services, involves complex and lengthy sales negotiations. In addition, sales of such complex services may require extensive after-sale support. In these situations, sales representatives may operate as part of a team of sales representatives and experts from other departments. Sales representatives receive valuable technical assistance from these experts. For example, those who sell data processing services might work with a systems engineer or computer scientist, and those who sell telephone services might receive technical assistance from a communications consultant. Teams enhance customer service and build strong long-term relationships with customers, resulting in increased sales.

Because of the length of time between the initial contact with a customer and the actual sale, representatives who sell complex technical services generally work with several customers simultaneously. Sales representatives must be well organized and efficient in scheduling their time.

Selling less complex services, such as linen supply or exterminating services, generally involves simpler and shorter sales negotiations.

A sales representative's job may likewise vary with the size of the employer. Those working for large companies generally are more specialized and are assigned territorial boundaries, a specific line of services, and their own accounts. In smaller companies, sales representatives may have broader responsibilities–administrative, marketing, or public relations, for example–in addition to their sales duties.

A sales representative often services a specific territory. A representative for a company offering services widely used by the general public, such as pest control, generally has numerous clients in a relatively small territory. On the other hand, a sales representative for a more specialized organization, such as a standardized testing service, may need to service several states to acquire an adequate customer base.

Services sales representatives held about 488,000 jobs in 1992. Over half were in firms providing business services, including computer and data processing, advertising, personnel supply, equipment rental and leasing, and mailing, reproduction, and stenographic services. Other sales representatives worked for firms that offer a wide range of other services, as the following chart shows.

Total	100%
Business services	53
Computer and data processing	10
Advertising	8
Personnel supply	7
Mailing, reproduction, and stenographic	3
Miscellaneous equipment rental and leasing	3
Other business services	22
Engineering and management	11
Personal	17
Amusement and recreation	5
Automotive repair	5
Membership organizations	4
Hotels and other lodging places	3
Motion pictures	2
Health	2
Education, public and private	2
Other services	6

TRAINING

Many employers require that services sales representatives have a college degree, but requirements may vary depending on the industry a particular company represents. Employers who market advertising services seek individuals with a college degree in advertising or marketing or a master's degree in business administration; companies that market educational services prefer individuals with an advanced degree in marketing or a related field.

Many hotels seek graduates from college hotel administration programs, and companies that sell computer services and telephone systems prefer sales representatives with a background in computer science or engineering. College courses in business, economics, communications, and marketing are helpful in obtaining other jobs as services sales representatives.

Employers may hire sales representatives with a high school diploma if they have a proven sales record. This is particularly true for those who sell nontechnical services, such as linen supply, exterminating, laundry, or funeral services.

Many firms conduct intensive training programs for their sales representatives. A sound training program covers the history of the business; origin development, and uses of the service; effective prospecting methods; presentation of the service; answering customer objections; creating customer demand; closing a sale; writing an order; company policies; and using technical support personnel.

Sales representatives also may attend seminars on a wide range of subjects given by outside or in-house training institutions. These sessions acquaint them with new services and products and help them maintain and update their sales techniques, and may include motivational or sensitivity training to make sales representatives more effective in dealing with people. They generally receive training in the use of computers and communications technology in order to increase their productivity.

Very large companies often prefer to hire sales representatives directly out of college, while smaller companies often prefer to hire individuals with a proven sales record. Smaller companies generally prefer not to incur the expense of providing formal training programs for their sales representatives.

In order to be successful, sales representatives should have a pleasant, outgoing personality and good rapport with people. They must be highly motivated, well organized, and efficient. Good grooming and a neat appearance are essential, as are self-confidence, reliability, and the ability to effectively communicate. Sales representatives should be self-starters who have the ability to work under pressure to meet sales goals.

Sales representatives who have good sales records and leadership ability may advance to supervisory and managerial positions.

Frequent contact with business people in other firms provides sales workers with leads about job openings, enhancing advancement opportunities.

JOB OUTLOOK

Employment of services sales representatives, as a group, is expected to grow faster than the average for all occupations through the year 2005 in response to growth of the services industries that employ them. However, the projected growth of particular services industries varies, and employment of services sales representatives will not keep pace with industry growth due to downsizing of the sales force in many services industries, and the growing use of various technologies, such as voice mail, cellular telephones, and laptop computers, that increase sales workers' productivity. For example, the continued growth in factory and office automation should lead to much faster than average employment growth for computer and data processing services sales representatives, while faster than average growth is expected among sales representatives in health services. Average growth is projected for representatives who sell advertising, while slower than average employment growth is projected for representatives who sell educational services.

In addition to the jobs generated by this growth, openings will occur each year because of the need to replace sales workers who transfer to other occupations or leave the labor force. Each year, many sales representatives discover that they are unable to earn enough money at selling and leave the occupation. Turnover generally is higher among representatives who sell nontechnical services, since they have invested less time and effort in specialized training.

Prospective services sales representatives with a college background or a proven sales record should have the best job opportunities.

SALARIES

In 1992, the median annual income for full-time advertising sales representatives was over $26,000, while representatives selling other business services earned nearly $30,000. Earnings of representatives who sold technical services generally were higher than earnings of those who sold nontechnical services.

Earnings of experienced sales representatives depend on performance. Successful sales representatives who establish a strong customer base can earn more than managers in their firm. Some sales representatives earn well over $100,000 a year.

According to a 1991 survey conducted by TPF & C, a Towers Perrin company, annual earnings of services sales representatives in Fortune 500 companies ranged from about $39,000 for beginners to $60,000 for those with five years of experience. Experienced sales workers responsible for key clients averaged over $70,000 a year.

Sales representatives work on different types of compensation plans. Some get a straight salary; others are paid solely on a commission basis, a percentage of the dollar value of their sales. Most firms use a combination of salary and commissions.

Some services sales representatives receive a base salary plus incentive pay that adds 50 to 70 percent to the sales representative's base salary. In addition to the same benefits package received by other employees of the firm, outside sales representatives have expense accounts to cover meals and travel, and some drive a company car. Many employers offer bonuses, including vacation time, trips, and prizes, for sales that exceed company quotas.

Because sales are affected by changing economic conditions and consumer and business expectations, earnings may fluctuate widely from year to year.

RELATED FIELDS

Services sales representatives must have sales ability and a knowledge of the service they sell. Workers in other occupations that require these skills include real estate agents, insurance agents, securities and financial services sales representatives, manufacturers' and wholesale sales representatives, and travel agents.

INTERVIEW

Le Anne Coury
Assistant Director of Sales

LeAnne Coury has been in the hotel and sales business for 20 years. She works at the Quality Suites Hotel, a national chain. In her particular property, she has 207 suites and 3 meeting rooms for which she is responsible.

What the Job's Really Like

"Every day is different, not like in some jobs where the work can get monotonous. The hotel industry isn't like that. You might come in in the morning with a plan to work on something specific, then something comes up and you end up doing something else. The meeting planners for a large group convention might come in and want to discuss details with you, so you put your other work on hold for a while.

"Basically, the way it works in the sales end of things is that you're out looking for new business and staying on top of your current business. We look for corporate customers and we want to stay in touch on a regular basis.

"I'm on the phone a lot, checking details, taking care of rooming lists. There are always a lot of details and you have to follow through on promises you make. For example, if you promised to hold 10 two-bedded suites for them, you have to make sure that's what got booked, not 10 king suites. And with conferences, you need to follow up on AV equipment or registration tables, that sort of thing.

"I'm up and down a lot, too; I'm not just always sitting at a desk. I walk around the hotel, double check on my groups, make sure they're happy.

"As I said, every day is new because you're working with different people all the time. That's what I think makes it fun.

"But, as with any job, there are always some downsides. Sometimes you get bogged down with paperwork, but if you're an organized person you should be able to stay on top of it. It's not too bad.

"Another thing in this business, a hotel never closes, so your hours won't always be the best sometimes. You could be working nights, weekends. However, I think once you put enough time in, you can move into some of the positions where you don't have such a messed-up schedule. With a smaller hotel, it's a little easier.

"But the advantages far outweigh the disadvantages. In sales you're working with some high-energy people in an up kind of atmosphere. We have bells on our desk and when we book something we ring our bells. Doing sales blitzes is lots of fun, too. We do ours with a theme. The most recent one was called "We're Fishin' for Your Business." We had special shirts with fish printed on them, as well as our logo. We also put together what we call a "blitz bag." They're plastic bags that we stuff with all sorts of promotional items, such as coasters, rulers, calculators. Then, unannounced, we go out and visit big office buildings. We just walk in and tell them we'd like to be able to work with them, that we're 'fishin' for their business.' We recently hit about three or four hundred businesses in this area. It's a good way to get leads and get your name out there.

"We laugh and have a good time at our job. It's fun to go to work. I've never gotten up in the morning and dreaded going in."

How LeAnne Coury Got Started

"Right out of high school I worked for a Chamber of Commerce, for the convention and sales department. That's where I first got into the convention end. I got to see how they booked the whole city, how they go after major conventions. I worked with booking blocks of hotel rooms city-wide versus working in one specific hotel.

"After about a year there, I realized I wouldn't have a chance for advancement. Hotels offer better opportunities and more money. The experience I got with the Chamber of Commerce translated well into hotel work.

"I took a position as a sales and catering secretary at the Red Lion Hotel in Oregon. They had about 75 very upscale hotels. I was there only six months and learned everything I could. Then I applied for a position in another hotel that I saw was under construction about two hours away. I sat with the general manager in the coffee shop for an hour or so. He ended up calling me and offering me the sales and convention manager position. It was on a trial basis because of my age; I was only 20 at the time. The drinking age was 21, so they had legal issues to deal with about my selling liquor. That was a great job. They could seat 1,000 and I pretty much ran all of that. I stayed there for three and a half years, but then an opportunity came up for me to go back to Red Lion as the sales and catering manager. It turned out to be a good move for me, more money, more knowledge. After three years I moved south, to Alabama, but there weren't as many hotel opportunities there for me, so I went into the legal field for a while and worked as a legal secretary.

"But I missed the hotels. It's usually something you either love or hate, there's no in between. I finally found a job in Mobile and traveled between five different states, promoting the hotel.

"In 1990 I started at the Quality Suites Hotel in Deerfield Beach, Florida. My first position was as sales and catering manager, and later I moved up to my current position, assistant director of sales. The next step up for me would be as director of sales, then I could even think about moving into a general manager position. The opportunities are there and they're willing to train you."

Expert Advice

"If you're going to be in this industry, you have to be a people person and have a happy personality. You have to be able to always have a smile on your face, and if a guest or a customer is dissatisfied, you have to be able to handle it. You don't ever want to lose business.

"You have to be a team player, too. If the restaurant gets busy, for example, I'll go over and help them out there. If someone needs help, then that's what you do. Our job descriptions aren't rigidly set. But it's fun to do something different once in a while.

"Another thing, when you're looking for work, you'll probably be better off working for a hotel that is corporate owned rather than a family-owned franchise. There'll be more opportunities for you to move up and probably better salaries.

"But don't get discouraged when you're starting out at the bottom. For example, a position at the front desk might not be the highest paying job, but it's a good way to learn."

●　　　●　　　●

FOR MORE INFORMATION

For details about employment opportunities for services sales representatives, contact employers who sell services in your area.

For information on careers and scholarships in hotel management and sales contact:

The American Hotel and Motel Association (AH&MA)
Information Center
1201 New York Avenue, N.W.
Washington, DC 20005-3931

CHAPTER 3

Manufacturers' and Wholesale Sales Representatives

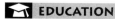 **EDUCATION**
B.A. Recommended

$$$ SALARY/EARNINGS
$16,000 to $60,000

OVERVIEW

Computers, compact discs, and articles of clothing are among the thousands of products bought and sold each day. Manufacturers', brokers, and wholesale sales representatives are an important part of this process. They market their company's products to manufacturers, wholesale and retail establishments, government agencies, and other institutions. Regardless of the type of product they sell, the primary duties of these sales representatives are to interest wholesale and retail buyers and purchasing agents in their merchandise and ensure that any questions or concerns of current clients are addressed. Sales reps also provide advice to clients on how to increase sales. (Retail sales workers, who sell directly to consumers, are discussed in Chapter 1.)

Depending on where they work, these sales representatives have different job titles. Many of those representing manufacturers are referred to as manufacturers' representatives and those employed by wholesalers generally are called sales representatives.

Those selling technical products, for both manufacturers and wholesalers, are usually called industrial sales workers or sales engineers. In addition to those employed directly by firms, manufacturers' agents are self-employed sales workers who contract their services to all types of companies.

Manufacturers' and wholesale sales representatives spend much of their time traveling to and visiting with prospective buyers and current clients. During a sales call, they discuss the customers' needs and suggest how their merchandise or services can meet those needs. They may show samples or catalogs that describe items their company stocks and inform customers about prices, availability, and how their products can save money and improve productivity. In addition, because of the vast number of manufacturers and wholesalers selling similar products, they try to emphasize the unique qualities of the products and services offered by their company. They also take orders and resolve any problems or complaints with the merchandise.

These sales representatives have additional duties as well. For example, sales engineers, who are among the most highly trained sales workers, typically sell products whose installation and optimal use require a great deal of technical expertise and support products such as material handling equipment, numerical-control machinery, and computer systems. In addition to providing information on their firm's products, these workers help prospective and current buyers with technical problems. For example, they may recommend improved materials and machinery for a firm's manufacturing process, draw up plans of proposed machinery layouts, and estimate cost savings from the use of their equipment. They present this information and negotiate the sale, a process that may take several months.

Afterwards sales engineers will keep close contact with the client to assure the client renews the contract. Sales engineers may work with engineers in their own companies, adapting products to a customer's special needs.

Increasingly, sales representatives who lack technical expertise work as a team with a technical expert. For example, a sales representative will make the preliminary contact with customers, introduce his or her company's product, and close the sale. However, the technically trained person will attend the sales presentation to explain and answer technical questions and concerns. In this way, the sales representative is able to spend more time maintaining and soliciting accounts and less time acquiring technical knowledge. After the sale, sales representatives may make frequent follow-up visits to ensure that the equipment is functioning properly and may even help train customers' employees to operate and maintain new equipment. They may be equipped with a portable computer so they can have instant access to technical, sales, and other information while they are with a customer.

Those selling consumer goods often suggest how and where their merchandise should be displayed. Working with retailers, they may help arrange promotional programs and advertising.

Obtaining new accounts is an important part of the job. Sales representatives follow leads suggested by other clients, from advertisements in trade journals, and from participation in trade shows and conferences. At times, they make unannounced visits to potential clients. In addition, they may spend a lot of time meeting with and entertaining prospective clients during evenings and weekends.

Sales representatives also analyze sales statistics, prepare reports, and handle administrative duties, such as filing their expense account reports, scheduling appointments, and making travel plans. They study literature about new and existing products and monitor the sales, prices, and products of their competitors.

In addition to all these duties, manufacturers' agents must manage their businesses. This requires organizational skills as well as knowledge of accounting, marketing, and administration.

Some manufacturers' and wholesale sales representatives have large territories and do considerable traveling. Because a sales region may cover several states, they may be away from home for several days or weeks at a time. Others work near their home base and do most of their traveling by automobile. Due to the nature of the work and the amount of travel, sales representatives typically work more than 40 hours per week.

Selling pharmaceuticals and medical equipment is discussed in Chapter 4.

TRAINING

The background needed for sales jobs varies by product line and market. As the number of college graduates has increased and the job requirements have become more technical and analytical, most firms have placed a greater emphasis on a strong educational background. Nevertheless, many employers still hire individuals with previous sales experience who do not have a college degree.

In fact, for some consumer products, sales ability, personality, and familiarity with brands are more important than a degree.

On the other hand, firms selling industrial products often require a degree in science or engineering in addition to some sales experience. In general, companies are looking for the best and brightest individuals who display the personality and desire necessary to sell.

Many companies have formal training programs for beginning sales representatives that last up to two years. However, most businesses are accelerating these programs to reduce costs and expedite the return from training. In some programs, trainees rotate among jobs in plants and offices to learn all phases of production, installation, and distribution of the product. In others, trainees take formal classroom instruction at the plant, followed by on-the-job training under the supervision of a field sales manager.

In some firms, new workers are trained by accompanying more experienced workers on their sales calls. As these workers gain familiarity with the firm's products and clients, they are given increasing responsibility until they are eventually assigned their own territory. As businesses experience greater competition, increased pressure is placed upon sales representatives to produce faster.

These workers must stay abreast of new merchandise and the changing needs of their customers. They may attend trade shows where new products are displayed or conferences and conventions where they meet with other sales representatives and clients to discuss new product developments. In addition, many companies sponsor meetings of their entire sales force where presentations are made on sales performance, product development, and profitability.

Manufacturers' and wholesale sales representatives should be goal-oriented, persuasive, and able to work both as a team member and independently. A pleasant personality and appearance, the ability to get along well with people, and problem-solving skills are important as well. Patience and perseverance are also needed because completing a sale can take several months. Because these workers may be on their feet for long periods and may have to carry heavy sample cases, some physical stamina is necessary.

Sales representatives should also enjoy traveling because much of their time is spent visiting current and prospective clients.

Frequently, promotion takes the form of an assignment to a larger account or territory where commissions are likely to be greater. Experienced sales representatives may move into jobs as sales trainers–workers who train new employees on selling techniques and company policies and procedures. Those who have good sales records and leadership ability may advance to sales supervisor or district manager.

In addition to advancement opportunities within a firm, some go into business for themselves as manufacturers' agents. Others find opportunities in buying, purchasing, advertising, or marketing research.

JOB OUTLOOK

Employment of manufacturers' and wholesale sales representatives is expected to grow more slowly than the average for all occupations through the year 2005 due to technological advances and changing business practices. Despite some growth in demand for sales representatives, most job openings will result from the need to replace workers who transfer to other occupations or leave the labor force.

Electronic data interchange (EDI) is used by a growing number of organizations. EDI enables computers to communicate with each other, making ordering and reordering goods from suppliers quicker and easier than ever before. EDI has the potential to substantially reduce the need for sales representatives when paired with other advances, such as point of sale inventory systems, which read the bar codes on merchandise and adjust inventory according to sales volume, or expert system software, which can predict sales trends.

In addition to the technological innovations that may affect employment demand, some of the largest companies are using their market power to negotiate directly with suppliers, bypassing sales representatives entirely.

At present, however, the majority of firms find it impractical to spend the amount of money required to operate such a complex system and many do not possess the negotiating power necessary to bypass the sales representative. In addition, smaller retailers who rely on their reputation for selling specialty and fashionable items or establishments that routinely change the lines they carry may not want to deal with an automated system that reduces their flexibility and diversity. For example, the use of automated reordering might be practical for a large grocery store that consistently stocks the same merchandise. However, this technology would be unsuitable for a small high fashion clothing retailer that changes inventory depending on the season and the latest trend.

Those interested in this occupation should keep in mind that direct selling opportunities in manufacturing are likely to be best for products with strong demand, such as consumer products or computers and related supplies and equipment. Furthermore, jobs will be most plentiful in small wholesale firms because a growing number of these companies will rely on wholesalers and manufacturers' agents to market their products as a way to control their costs and expand their customer base.

Opportunities for manufacturers' agents may be affected more adversely than other sales representatives by the changes in business practices, and, as a result, most independent sales representatives will work for smaller firms. These representatives will benefit from the increased consumption of imported goods because it is often more cost efficient for importers to delegate their sales responsibilities than to hire a sales force.

Employment opportunities and earnings may fluctuate from year to year because sales are affected by changing economic conditions, legislative issues, and consumer preferences. Prospects will be best for those with the appropriate knowledge or technical expertise as well as the personal traits necessary for successful selling.

SALARIES

Compensation methods vary significantly by the type of firm and product sold. However, most employers use a combination of salary and commission or salary plus bonus. Commissions are usually based on the amount of sales, whereas bonuses may depend on individual performance, on the performance of all sales workers in the group or district, or on the company's performance.

Median annual earnings of full-time manufacturers' and wholesale sales representatives were about $32,000 in 1992. The bottom 10 percent earned less than $16,400; the top 10 percent earned more than $62,000 per year. Earnings vary by experience and the type of goods or services sold.

In addition to their earnings, sales representatives are usually reimbursed for expenses such as transportation costs, meals, hotels, and entertaining customers. They often receive benefits such as health and life insurance, a pension plan, vacation and sick leave, personal use of a company car, and frequent flyer mileage. Some companies offer incentives such as free vacation trips or gifts for outstanding sales workers.

Unlike those working directly for a manufacturer or wholesaler, manufacturers' agents work strictly on commission. Depending on the type of product they are selling, their experience in the field, and the number of clients, their earnings can be significantly higher or lower than those working in direct sales. In addition, because manufacturers' agents are self-employed, they must pay their own travel and entertainment expenses as well as provide for their own benefits, which can be a significant cost.

RELATED FIELDS

Manufacturers' and wholesale sales representatives must have sales ability and knowledge of the products they sell. Other occupations that require similar skills are retail sales, real estate, insurance sales, medical sales (see Chapters 4 and 9), food services (see Chapter 9), and securities sales workers, as well as wholesale and retail buyers.

INTERVIEW
Pat Reese
Flower Broker

Pat Reese is a pioneer as a broker in cut flowers. When he started as

a broker 15 years ago, he was one of the first in the industry.

What the Job's Really Like

"Brokers and wholesalers perform similar functions. They purchase stock directly from growers or importers and supply florists with fresh flowers, decorative plants, and other related items. However, how they work with the florists differs a great deal.

"Based on the estimated need of their regular customers, wholesalers buy a certain quantity of flowers each week at a price determined by the growers or importers. This could be, for example, 1000 boxes of fresh carnations (with 600 carnations to a box), 500 cases of pom poms, and 50 dozen roses. At the beginning of the week, when the florists' coolers need replenishing and the wholesalers' stock is fresh, the wholesalers add in their expenses and a profit to the price given to the florists. As the week goes by and the flowers are no longer in peak condition, the wholesaler will adjust the price downward, according to what the market can bear. The wholesalers' earning power can see a great deal of fluctuation.

"Wholesalers receive their flowers from their suppliers, and store them, usually in a refrigerated warehouse, provide them with any care and conditioning they need, then deliver them to the florists. The florists are usually located within an easy delivery distance from the wholesaler, most likely within a 50-mile radius.

"In addition to standing orders, wholesalers supply florists with special orders. They can send over one rare bird-of-paradise or a half-dozen orchids for a bride's bouquet.

"Brokers go directly to the grower or importer and get a price for a particular item. That price is set for the day and will not change. After adding on his profit margin to the price, the broker then, usually over the telephone, sells the stock to the florists. Only after he has actually sold the flowers will the broker go back to the grower and plant down his money, so to speak.

"This procedure, of selling stock at a guaranteed price, eliminates all risk for the broker. In addition, he is not responsible for warehousing and taking care of plants. He doesn't even have to get involved in shipping; the grower or importer can send the purchase overnight directly to the florist, who can be located anywhere in the country.

"On the surface, considering the benefits to the broker, it is surprising that there are any wholesalers in business. They have all the financial risk and most of the responsibility of keeping the flowers in good condition. A broker needs only a telephone and a good sales pitch.

"However, most retail florist shops prefer to work with local wholesalers. The florist can drop in, see what's in stock and pick out a few of this and a few of that. Wholesalers will handle special orders or spur-of-the moment deliveries. Wholesalers will also give the florist a call every morning and ask what he needs. The order is then placed on the truck and there by the afternoon. Brokers are not equipped to do this.

"The customers brokers deal with are usually large retail outlets that handle a large volume of business. They place orders on a weekly, or twice weekly, as opposed to daily basis. Many florists work with both brokers and wholesalers. They get their day-to-day orders through the wholesaler and go to brokers to supplement that with the larger orders they know in advance they're regularly going to need. For example, if a florist knows he'll regularly sell 100 carnations a week, he'll place that order through a broker. The other orders, such as for weddings or funerals, will go to the wholesaler.

How Pat Reese Got Started

"When I started there really was no one else doing this. It was all by the traditional wholesaling method. Now, of course, there are quite a few brokers. And what has happened is that many of the growers have seen what a brokering business can do and they have formed their own brokerage companies.

"I started out working with a floral publishing company as an advertising manager. I stayed with them for nine years, then went on to the flower-by-wire service business as a field representative with Teleflora. When I left Teleflora 15 years ago to become a broker, I was Vice President of Sales in California.

"After having spent almost 20 years of my adult life being in and around florist shops, I kept seeing a need for a more efficient system. I was running into disgruntled florists all the time who were upset with their local wholesalers for a hundred different reasons. At the same time the FAX machine was just starting to make its way in, and transportation was something I'd always been interested in, and it became a desire to find a different way. I wanted to build a better mousetrap. And I did.

"I took my idea to three former presidents of Teleflora and each one of them became a full partner in my company, which is called Floral International Xpress, or FIX. I was the operating officer and they were investors.

"Since then, I have bought out my investors and am now sole proprietor."

Expert Advice

"The first thing you should do if you're interested in this kind of career is to make sure you know the flower industry. When I plunged in, I already knew thousands of florists on a first-name basis and had a ready-made list of customers.

"You also have to have a good sales background, and for brokering, you need telemarketing skills. Most, if not all, of your selling will be done over the telephone. You need to know about distribution and also have a strong financial background.

"A source of start-up capital is also necessary, for both brokering and wholesaling, although the amount is usually smaller for the new broker. Brokers don't have overhead to worry about or warehouses or refrigeration or insurance and employees and delivery. They can work anywhere they can install a telephone.

"But for both professions, until you've established yourself with the growers and importers, you'll have to pay up front for the goods you purchase. There's always a gap of time before you get paid by the florists and you have to be able to cover yourself during that period."

● ● ●

FOR MORE INFORMATION

Information on manufacturers' agents is available from:

Sales and Marketing Management International
Statier Office Tower
Cleveland OH, 44115

Information on the floral industry can be obtained from the contacts listed at the end of Chapter 1.

CHAPTER 4 Medical Sales

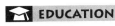 **EDUCATION**
B.A. Required

$$$ SALARY/EARNINGS
$35,000 to $60,000

OVERVIEW

There are three different categories within medical sales: pharmaceutical sales, medical surgical sales, and the sale of capital equipment. Typically, individual companies will deal with only one category, although some of the bigger companies, such as Johnson & Johnson or Baxter, operate all three divisions.

Pharmaceutical Sales

The pharmaceutical sales business is educational in scope. The medical sales rep would go to a doctor's office or a group practice for the primary purpose of explaining how a particular drug works and how it interacts with other drugs. The rep would explain what types of indications it has and what kinds of patients it works for.

Pharmaceutical sales reps are very important to the physician because they're the people who collect all the research that has been done on a particular drug and highlight the important information.

This aspect of medical sales is not sales-oriented in the true sense of the word; reps are not asking for an order. They are trying to explain why their product works better than another company's product. The sales come when the physician prescribes that particular medication to a patient.

The pharmacy is the entity that will actually buy the product from the manufacturer and the pharmacist stocks his or her shelves based on demand.

With pharmaceutical sales, it's a numbers game. Productivity measurements are activity oriented. Supervisors might tell reps to call on 10 or so general practitioners a day in a particular territory. The more calls a rep makes, the more chances the physicians will prescribe the product, and the more sales there'll be down the road.

Typically, pharmaceutical sales territories are very small. Reps can usually live in the same city in which their contacts are, although it might be necessary to relocate when they first land their new job.

TRAINING FOR PHARMACEUTICAL SALES REPRESENTATIVES.

In this area in medical sales, the basic requirement is a four-year degree. Unlike other areas of medical sales, the course of study is open, no specific major is required. Certainly someone with a good science background would not be turned away, but surprisingly, sciences are not required.

Companies usually look for candidates who have demonstrated in their background the capacity to learn new information. They look for high GPAs and graduates who have had a lot of experience with extracurricular activities. The ideal candidate is an outgoing people person.

On-the-job training is provided by most companies. New reps learn all about the companies' products and usually start off their territory under the wing of an experienced rep.

The training period usually runs from six months to a year, depending on the company. The first month would be spent at the home office in a classroom setting. Trainees would probably spend another month in another rep's territory and then they'd spend another month in their own territories with different reps working with them. After the reps have gotten their feet wet they might be required to spend additional time back at the home office.

Advancement opportunities are good within this field. There are usually several layers of management positions into which a sales rep can move. Most pharmaceutical companies, as well as med/surg companies (discussed later in this chapter), have direct district managers, regional managers, division managers, training positions, and other related areas to which successful reps can be promoted.

SALARIES FOR PHARMACEUTICAL SALES REPRESENTATIVES.
Normally, sales reps in this area of medical sales are paid a fairly high base salary in the $35,000 to $60,000 a year range. This depends on the company and how new the rep is to the business. As the rep gains experience and his or her productivity level increases, so does the base salary.

Pharmaceutical sales rep are also typically paid a yearly bonus. Companies calculate this bonus by measuring the percentage of increase in retail sales. These figures are supplied to the manufacturer by distributors. Usually, pharmaceutical companies sell their products to distributors and distributors handle the sales to the pharmacies. The sales figures are tracked from the pharmacies in a rep's specific territory.

A downside to this method of tracking is that many reps feel that the system isn't as accurate as it should be.

There is generally a cap to the bonus; most companies don't have open-ended commission structures. If, for example, the sales goal for a new drug is 1000 units, then the rep will make the same bonus whether he sells 1000 units or 2000. The bonus can amount to $6,000 to $10,000 per year.

Other perks usually include excellent health insurance programs, pension plans, company cars, and all travel and work-related expenses paid.

Jobs in all areas of medical sales are very competitive.

 **EDUCATION**
B.A. Required

$$$ SALARY/EARNINGS
$50,000 to $100,000

Medical Surgical Sales (Med/Surg)

This area covers the sale of products made by medical surgical companies. Typically these are single-use products such as bandages, surgical dressings, sutures, syringes, or surgical gloves.

The med/surg sales rep sells these products directly to the hospital or physicians' office. Although these reps play an educational role similar to that of the pharmaceutical sales rep, their main goal is to get the order.

Med/surg reps generally travel about 10 percent more a year than pharmaceutical reps do. Their territories are usually larger and perhaps once a week they would find themselves making overnight trips. Out of five days, two could be spent on the road away from home.

TRAINING FOR MED/SURG SALES REPRESENTATIVES.

A four-year degree plus previous sales experience (in any field) is usually the requirement to get into this area. While the pharmaceutical sales rep can start off with just the bachelor's degree–the work is more educational in nature than straight selling–the med/surg rep needs to have proven sales experience.

Companies looking to hire new med/surg reps prefer to take on someone who was in the top 10 percent of their previous sales organization. This is not an area for a beginner.

SALARIES FOR MED/SURG SALES REPRESENTATIVES.

Med/Surg sales reps are usually paid on a salary plus commission basis. Although it varies from company to company, it is usually a 50/50 split.

The total compensation package has a wide spread, but usually runs from $50,000 to $100,000 a year. The straight salary could range from $25,000 to $50,000, and commissions can run up to $50,000 or more.

Because the products a med/surg rep sells are usually designed as "throw-aways", the opportunities for repeat sales are very high.

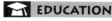 EDUCATION
B.A. Required

 SALARY/EARNINGS
$50,000 to $200,000

Capital Equipment

Capital equipment covers large, and often expensive, pieces of equipment such as lasers, sterilizers, surgical lights, hospital beds, and x-ray machines. Typically a capital equipment company would manufacture and sell just one product.

The territory a capital equipment sales rep would cover tends to be much larger than the other two types of medical sales position mentioned earlier in this chapter. Pharmaceutical sales reps usually focus on the city in which they live; med/surg reps might cover two or three states. But a capital equipment sales rep could be responsible for sales in 20, 30, or even all 50 states, as well as a variety of countries abroad.

Although a lot of business in the planning stages is done over the telephone, when it comes down to the actual selling, the capital equipment sales reps must be on the road most of the year. This is not a job for those who prefer to stay close to home; the travel required in this category is extensive.

Capital equipment companies usually hire only two to four sales reps, and with only three or four major companies producing each product, the competition isn't as fierce as in the other two categories.

Hospitals usually plan out their capital equipment budgets at least a year in advance and this information is available to sales reps.

TRAINING FOR CAPITAL EQUIPMENT SALES REPRESENTATIVES. In order to land a job as a capital equipment sales rep, previous specific medical sales experience is required in addition to a four-year college degree. Reps with previous medical sales experience will already have extensive hospital contacts and this edge is important to employers.

Typically, representatives start out in pharmaceutical or med/surg sales, then work their way up to capital equipment sales.

Advancement possibilities in this area of medical sales is very low. A company might have only four reps and one manager, so this often does not leave room for regular promotions.

SALARIES FOR CAPITAL EQUIPMENT SALES REPRESENTATIVES. Although the opportunities for repeat sales are limited (hospitals tend to go through more bandages than they do beds) the income for sales reps in this category is generally the highest in medical sales.

A rep could make a $10,000 to $20,000 commission on the sale of just one piece of $100,000 equipment. Depending on the cost of the equipment a rep is selling, just a few sales a year would be enough to provide an attractive annual income in the $100,000 to $200,000 range.

Generally, income for capital equipment sales reps comes solely from commissions.

JOB OUTLOOK

Employment of manufacturers' and wholesale sales representatives is expected to grow more slowly than the average for all occupations through the year 2005 due to technological advances and changing business practices. Competition for sales positions within the medical sales field will continue to increase as more and more companies consolidate and merge.

Despite some growth in demand for sales representatives, most job openings will result from the need to replace workers who transfer to other occupations or leave the labor force.

More information on jobs with manufacturers' and wholesale sales reps is offered in Chapter 3.

RELATED FIELDS

Medical sales representatives must have sales ability and knowledge of the products they sell. Other occupations that require similar skills are retail sales, manufacturers' and wholesale sales and marketing, real estate, insurance sales, food services (see Chapter 9), and securities sales workers, as well as wholesale and retail buyers.

For more information about careers in medical sales and marketing, turn to Chapter 9.

INTERVIEW
Chad Ellis
Med/Surg Account Executive

Chad Ellis has worked for Kimberly-Clark since 1985. He began his career with KC as a sales representative, then moved up to the positions of senior sales representative, account manager, and then to his current position as account executive. Although KC's headquarters are in Roswell, Georgia, Chad is based in Kentucky.

Kimberly-Clark's med/surg division sells surgical gowns, surgical drapes, sterilization wrap, and infection control products such as cover gowns.

What the Job's Really Like

"We have four different levels of sales positions in our company, and this is unique—with most companies you're usually a sales rep or a manager. Our company's entry-level sales positions are called sales representatives; then we have senior sales representatives; next is account managers; and then my position, account executives.

"The difference involves the level of responsibility at which you're selling. The sales rep is going to be geared to the hospital level. The senior sales rep is responsible for hospital accounts and also is responsible for some training of new sales representatives. An account manager would have those same responsibilities, plus be involved in some test marketing of new products, as well as calling on what we call group accounts. A group of hospitals would form a group account. The head office would make a decision on a product rather than just one hospital.

"My position, account executive, has all those responsibilities I mentioned, plus we have some national accounts responsibilities. We have some accounts that the decision for purchases for all the hospitals is made on a national basis. For example, HCA/Columbia, the biggest for-profit chain of hospitals in the United States, makes decisions for all their hospitals. So a local rep calling on an HCA Columbia Hospital in Texas has no influence on what the hospital buys. They're headquartered in Tennessee and that's where the decisions are made.

"We have 40 sales rep, 25 or 30 senior sales reps, 35 account managers, and only 5 people who are account executives.

"We also have another position called a sales associate. One of the hardest parts of our business is that it takes a long time to get someone trained and up to speed. And it's very expensive to do that. It could take almost a year to get someone in a position where they feel comfortable and can go out and sell something.

"One of the things we do is occasionally hire someone we call a sales associate. They don't even have a territory. We hire them and start training them and when a territory becomes open, they have to relocate. They are hired with that precondition in place. We'll have two or three sales associates at any one time.

"Marketing and sales departments are coexisting entities. We have a lot of people who move from sales into marketing. They're usually called product managers. They're responsible for a particular product. For example, surgical gowns. We have a product manager who is marketing director for surgical gowns. We have an integrated approach to all of our products. The marketing manager is in charge of the product, but we also have a product developer who is a scientist. Marketing covers design, manufacturing, distribution, and sales support of the product. They put together any literature on technical studies that are done, any type of sales collateral that would support the sales force.

"In addition to national accounts, I do have responsibility for individual hospital accounts, too, but I don't have as many accounts in my territory as a sales rep would have because I spend more of my time calling on a smaller number of national accounts or group headquarters.

"There is no typical day in this job. In a given month I probably spend 40 percent of my time with sales and 60 percent providing inservices and training.

"I train new reps. Typically, they would leave whatever territory they're in and come to me in Kentucky, either at a hotel or at my home office. Sometimes I might go to Georgia, where our headquarters are, to be a guest speaker for the trainees.

"I spend a good part of my time doing inservices, both in the operating room and in the Central Service Department of hospitals. The inservices are to keep hospital employees abreast of changes in the industry relative to things like OSHA standards.

"The sales cycle in a hospital is a very lengthy one. If I were starting in a new territory, the first thing I'd have to do is get to know all the key decision-makers at every account I have. There are three or four people I need to know, such as the operating room director and the director of labor and delivery.

"The problem is that these people aren't anxious to meet me at all. Their attitude is 'I'm happy with what I have, I don't need to see you' or 'I'm busy, go away.'

"It's one of those environments that can be discouraging and if people don't like to hear 'no,' then this is the wrong business for them. You're going to hear 'no' a lot, even if you've been in the business for a while.

"The med/surg business is a relationship business. You are trying to build up a level of trust so people have confidence in you and your company's products.

"You always make appointments first, there's no cold-calling in our business. But you do spend a lot of time on the phone. As far as travel goes, in my position there's not much, maybe four nights a month or one night a week.

"There are a lot of early mornings in this job. Operating room staff usually get in around 6:30 A.M. If you have an inservice, for example, you have to be there at 6:15 A.M. to get set up and be ready to go. You put in early hours and long hours. It's not a typical 40-hours-a-week job, more like 100 hours a week. And that's mainly because it's constantly on your mind and there's all sorts of paperwork to do and a lot of time putting together presentations and proposals. Even though we have a lot of stock company literature, you still have to prepare specific material for individual accounts.

"Because I spend less time on sales than my other duties, I earn a higher salary base, $51,000. I also get a commission, which averages about another $50,000. That's a good year. New people start at $27,000 for a base salary.

"I like that it's a relationship business. Like I say to our reps, 'we're just riding around visiting our friends.' I'm not fiscally responsible for my business, so I don't have any of the capital risk involved that I'd have if I were an entrepreneur.

"But when I get out there every morning, it's almost as if I've hung a sign that says Chad Ellis, Sole Proprietor. Because it is my business. The company gives me the resources and the money that I need to run my business and then they leave me alone. I can run things the way I want. As long as I'm producing the sales numbers they want to see, they're not going to complain about it.

"What I like the least is the health care environment we're in right now. Pricing is such an incredible issue. It takes a lot of hard work, tenacity, and persuasion to get hospitals to understand all the things that influence the cost of using a product. The price of a product and the cost of using it can be very different."

How Chad Ellis Got Started

"It was one of those things that happens by accident. I was finishing up my undergraduate degree in speech and math at Western Kentucky University in Bowling Green. My original plan was to be a school teacher and to coach sports. Then I realized it was going to be awfully tough to make a decent living that way.

"One of my former professors called me up and said he wanted to come by to talk to me. He offered me a double stipend to come back to college in the graduate communications program and teach a couple of courses, coach the speech and debate team, and help him do a research project for the state government. I couldn't turn that down.

"I spent a year there and got involved doing a lot of research related to corporate selling. During that year in graduate school I went to the library and picked out the names of 100 companies I thought I might like to work for. I sent out letters to all 100 companies and I got interviews with three: Procter & Gamble, Harcourt Brace, and Stewart Pharmaceuticals. That was in 1982.

"P&G had a sales position open in Indianapolis and I got the job right away. I look back at that and realize I was very lucky. I worked for them for three-and-a-half years before moving to Kimberly-Clark. At P&G I spent a year as a sales rep, a year as a corporate field trainer. I was gone five nights a week from home and that was murder.

"Then I was promoted to district manager. At that time they called an emergency meeting and told us they were selling the surg end of the business to another company. They were willing to transfer me to Milwaukee as a district manager, but I really preferred staying in Kentucky. They had a sales position in Lexington in their professional services division. Any time a consumer product that would have some type of medical application would come on the market–for example, Crest toothpaste–they would hire the professional services division to go out and call on dentists for a year to explain this new toothpaste formula and try to get them to recommend the product to their patients. I did it for three months and I was absolutely miserable.

"I got a call from a recruiter who knew of an opening at Kimberly-Clark–I'm sure he got my name from a list that P&G circulated to help us out–and the rest is history."

Expert Advice

"Pharmaceutical sales is more service-oriented than sales-oriented. If you're the type of person who wants to be the number one sales rep in the company, then pharmaceutical sales would probably not be for you. You don't get as much recognition as with other areas of medical sales. Plus they have hundreds of reps. You have more chance to shine in med surg or capital equipment.

"When you're starting your job hunt you need to know how to track down medical recruiters. You won't see them advertised in the Yellow Pages. To find them go to a hospital and ask the people in the purchasing department to give you some of the names of the reps that call on them. Then ask those people how they got their job and which headhunters they worked with.

"The recruiters don't want to waste their time with people who aren't qualified, so they go out and try to find them rather than waiting for someone to come to them. They try to entice an employee from one company to get them to take a job with another.

"Also, find someone who is in the business and tag along for a couple of days to get a feel for the work. Most people will be agreeable. I did that. You can get their names also by calling the hospitals.

"You can also go to a specific hospital and meet the materials manager or purchasing director and ask them to tell you what companies have job openings right now. They usually know these things, as well as what the companies are like and who the sales reps are. If they're not happy dealing with a particular company, then you know to avoid applying there. On the pharmaceutical side, you could call physicians' offices and talk to the office managers."

●   ●   ●

FOR MORE INFORMATION

For more detailed information on a career in medical sales, look for Chad Ellis' upcoming book, *Opportunities in Medical Sales Careers* (VGM Career Horizons).

The following publication is a journal that, among other key information, includes personnel promotions from many major companies.

Pharmaceutical Representative
Two Northfield Plaza
Northfield, Illinois 60093-1217

The following professional associations can provide more information about the field.

Pharmaceutical Service Representative Association
16195 N.W. Spyglass Drive
Beaverton, OR 97006

Health Industry Distributors Association (HIDA)
225 Reinekers Lane #650
Alexandria, VA 22314

CHAPTER 5 Travel Agents

EDUCATION
Other

$$$ SALARY/EARNINGS
$12,000 to $25,000

OVERVIEW

Out of all the industries worldwide, travel and tourism continue to grow at an astounding rate. In fact, according to the Travel Works for America Council, it is the second largest employer in the United States (the first being health services). Nearly everyone tries to take at least one vacation every year and many people travel frequently on business. Some travel for education or for that special honeymoon or anniversary trip.

Constantly changing air fares and schedules, a proliferation of vacation packages, and business/pleasure trip combinations make travel planning frustrating and time-consuming. Many travelers, therefore, turn to travel agents, who can make the best possible travel arrangements for them.

Depending on the needs of the client, travel agents give advice on destinations, make arrangements for transportation, hotel accommodations, car rentals, tours, and recreation, or plan the right vacation package or business/pleasure trip combination.

They may also advise on weather conditions, restaurants, and tourist attractions and recreation. For international travel, agents also provide information on customs regulations, required papers (passports, visas, and certificates of vaccination), and currency exchange rates. Travel agents may also plan conventions and other meetings; they are usually referred to as meeting planners.

Travel agents must learn about all the different destinations, modes of transportation, hotels, resorts, and cruises, then work to match their customers' needs with the services travel providers offer.

Travel agents generally work in an office and deal with customers in person or over the phone. But first of all, they listen to the needs of their customers, then try to develop the best package for each person. They work with affluent, sophisticated travelers, or first-timers such as students trying to save money and travel on a budget. They could book a simple, round-trip air ticket for a person traveling alone, or handle arrangements for hundreds of people traveling to attend a convention or conference.

Some travel agents are generalists; they handle any or all situations. Others specialize in a particular area such as cruise ships or corporate travel.

Travel agents gather information from different sources. They use computer databases, attend trade shows, and read trade magazines. They also visit resorts or locations to get first-hand knowledge about a destination.

They have to keep up with rapidly changing fares and rates, and they have to know who offers the best packages and service. Their most important concern is the satisfaction of their client.

Most travel agents are offered "fam" trips to help familiarize them with a particular cruise line, safari adventure, exclusive resort, or ecological tour. These trips are offered free to the travel agent so they can "test-drive" a destination before suggesting it to their customers. Travel providers understand that a travel agent is more likely to sell what he or she knows and has enjoyed. Travel agents also receive discounted travel on other business trips, as well as on their own vacations.

Travel agents often base recommendations on their own travel experiences or those of colleagues or clients. Travel agents may visit hotels, resorts, and restaurants to judge, firsthand, their comfort, cleanliness, and quality of food and service.

The downside, however, according to many travel agents, is that they seldom have enough free time to do all the traveling they would like. They are often tied to their desks, especially during peak travel periods such as the summer or important busy holidays.

And the work can be frustrating at times. Customers might not always know what they want, or their plans can change, and as a result, the travel agent might have to cancel or reroute destinations that had already been set.

Travel agents also promote their services. They present slides or movies to social and special interest groups, arrange advertising displays, and suggest company-sponsored trips to business managers.

More than nine out of ten salaried agents worked for travel agencies.

TRAINING

Formal or specialized training is becoming increasingly important for travel agents since few agencies are willing to train people on the job. Many vocational schools offer 3- to 12-week full-time programs, as well as evening and Saturday programs. Travel courses are also offered in public adult education programs and in community and four-year colleges. A few colleges offer a bachelor's and a master's degree in travel and tourism.

Although few college courses relate directly to the travel industry, a college education is sometimes desired by employers. Courses in computer science, geography, foreign languages, and history are most useful. Courses in accounting and business management also are important, especially for those who expect to manage or start their own travel agencies. Several home-study courses provide a basic understanding of the travel industry.

The American Society of Travel Agents (ASTA) and the Institute of Certified Travel Agents offer a travel correspondence course. Travel agencies also provide on-the-job training for their employees, a significant part of which consists of computer instruction. These computer skills are required by employers to operate airline reservation systems.

Travel experience is an asset since personal knowledge about a city or foreign country often helps to influence clients' travel plans. Experience as an airline reservation agent also is a good background for a travel agent. Travel agents need good selling skills–they must be pleasant and patient and able to gain the confidence of clients.

Some employees start as reservation clerks or receptionists in travel agencies. With experience and some formal training, they can take on greater responsibilities and eventually assume travel agent duties. In agencies with many offices, travel agents may advance to office manager or to other managerial positions.

Experienced travel agents can take an advanced course, leading to the designation of Certified Travel Counselor, offered by the Institute of Certified Travel Agents. The institute awards a certificate to those completing an 18-month part-time course. It also offers certification, called designation of competence, in North American, Western European, Caribbean, or South Pacific tours.

Those who plan meetings also may be designated as Certified Meeting Professional (CMP). The CMP exam is administered by the Convention Liaison Council. To qualify to take the exam, a candidate must be employed in a meeting management position and have at least three years of meeting planning experience.

Those who start their own agencies generally have experience in an established agency. They must generally gain formal supplier or corporation approval before they can receive commissions. Suppliers or corporations are organizations of airlines, shiplines, or rail lines. The Airlines Reporting Corporation, for example, is the approving body for airlines. To gain approval, an agency must be in operation, be financially sound, and employ at least one experienced manager/travel agent.

There are no federal licensing requirements for travel agents. However, Rhode Island requires licensing, and Ohio, Hawaii, and California require registration. In California, travel agents not approved by a corporation are required to have a license.

JOB OUTLOOK

Employment of travel agents is expected to grow much faster than the average for all occupations through the year 2005. Many job openings will arise as new agencies open and existing agencies expand, but most will occur as experienced agents transfer to other occupations or leave the labor force.

Spending on travel is expected to increase significantly through the year 2005. As business activity expands, so will business-related travel. Employment of managerial, professional specialty, and sales representative occupations–those who do most business travel–is projected to grow rapidly.

Also, with rising incomes, more people are expected to travel on vacation and to do so more frequently than in the past. In fact, many people take more than one vacation a year.

Charter flights and larger, more efficient planes have brought air transportation within the budgets of more people. So has the easing of government regulation of air fares and routes, by fostering greater competition among airlines to offer better and more affordable service. In addition, American travel agents organize tours for the growing number of foreign visitors. Although most travel agencies now have automated reservation systems, this has not weakened demand for travel agents.

The travel industry generally is sensitive to economic downturns and political crises, when travel plans are likely to be deferred. Therefore, the number of job opportunities fluctuates.

SALARIES FOR TRAVEL AGENTS

Salaries vary according to the region in which you work and your experience. Depending on the agency, you could start out on an hourly wage or a yearly salary. Some travel agents prefer to work on a commission basis. That way, the more trips they sell, the more money they earn. A salary plus commission is the best combination with which to work.

Travel agents who are good salespeople can also earn bonuses or more free or discounted trips. If your pay is initially low, it can be offset by this added benefit.

Experience, sales ability, and the size and location of the agency determine the salary of a travel agent. According to a Louis Harris survey, conducted for *Travel Weekly Magazine*, the 1992 annual earnings of travel agents were as follows:

Less than 1 year experience–$12,428

From 1 to 3 years–$15,610

From 3 to 5 years–$17,975

From 5 to 10 years–$20,775

More than 10 years–$25,007

Salaried agents usually have standard benefits, such as insurance coverage and paid vacations, that self-employed agents must provide for themselves.

Earnings of travel agents who own their agencies depend mainly on commissions from airlines and other carriers, cruise lines, tour operators, and lodging places. Commissions for domestic travel arrangements, cruises, hotels, sightseeing tours, and car rentals are about 10 percent of the total sale; and for international travel, about 11 percent. They may also charge clients a service fee for the time and expense involved in planning a trip.

RELATED FIELDS

Other workers with similar duties include secretaries, tour guides, airline reservation agents, rental clerks, real estate agents, insurance agents, securities and financial services sales representatives, and manufacturers' and wholesale sales representatives.

INTERVIEW

Vivian Portela Buscher
Travel Agent

Vivian Portela Buscher started out as a ticket agent and in passenger services for the airlines, then moved to a well-known cruise line as a booking agent. It was a natural progression for her to become a travel agent specializing in cruise travel and she has worked for the same agency now since 1987.

What the Job's Really Like

"I work Monday through Friday, and because our agency is open from 9:00 A.M. to 9:00 P.M., I get to choose my hours during the day. Most people prefer to work earlier hours, but I don't. I work from 10:30 A.M. to 7:00 P.M.

"Basically, what I do is this: people call me who have an interest in taking a cruise vacation and I find for them the right cruise at the right price. I think of it more as a matching game rather than a selling situation. My office doesn't call anyone asking them to buy a cruise; everyone calls us.

"I enjoy travel a lot and it's nice to be able to talk about it all day long and to help people find the right travel experience. There's a lot of satisfaction when someone calls me back and tells me that the cruise was exactly as I had described it and that it was the best vacation of his or her life.

"You also get to travel yourself, to sample all the cruises to be more informed. I've been to St. Thomas, San Juan, Nassau, Grand Caymen, Jamaica, and St. Martin, to name just a few.

"We also get to attend a lot of luncheons and dinners and other inaugural activities to view the new ships.

"It's an office with a very high call volume. And there is always a lot of new information to learn, a lot of intensive studying you have to do to acquire all the product knowledge about all the different cruise lines and packages."

How Vivian Portela Buscher Got Started

"It's easy for me to advise other people about travel because it's something I like to do. I specifically chose to be a travel agent because working with the airlines had been becoming difficult. You had to wait a long time to gain seniority and to have a comfortable work schedule with Saturdays and Sundays off. Plus, with so many airlines going out of business, there are a lot of unemployed people in the industry. The airline I worked for folded ten years ago and I was happy to switch. I was looking for a job that would still be in the travel industry but that would be more secure and with normal hours.

"When I went to college I studied air carrier management and received a bachelor's degree in transportation management. My experience with the airlines and then with the cruise line also was important in preparing me. The rest I picked up through on-the-job training."

Expert Advice

"I think it's important to go to college and to get as much training as you can, and then to apply to work for an agency where you can get experience. Even if you get experience without going to school, it's very competitive. Sometimes the person with the most education will get the job over someone with equal experience."

INTERVIEW

Mary Fallon Miller
Travel Agent

Mary Fallon Miller started her career as a travel agent in 1986 when she opened her own agency. In partnership with a relative, she first focused on bus tours, transporting groups to see special events in her area. She later moved on to specialize in cruise travel.

What the Job's Really Like

"When you're just starting out, you're tied to the office and the computer a lot, but a newcomer would get to take at least one week a year, more once you've gained some seniority. The owners of a travel agency get to go on more "fam" trips, but if someone just starting out is seen as a productive member of the business, helping to build it, he or she would get more opportunities. You'll be the one they send on the "Cruise-a-Thon" or to the ski shows, and then you'll become your agency's representative.

"Beginners would probably start working side-by-side with someone more experienced in the agency. They might be placed in a specific department handling, for example, European travel, or cruises, or car rental and air fares. Much of their time will be spent coordinating and arranging details.

"It can be tricky keeping all the details accurate and being able to deal with what we call 'grumps and whiners.' There are people who get very nervous about their travel arrangements and they can complain and make your life miserable. But you have to be able to be compassionate–find out *why* they're so concerned. Maybe they had a bad experience in the past. You have to try to know as much about your client as possible.

"And there are times when things go wrong. There could be a snow-in at an airport and people miss their connections or someone in the family dies and they have to cancel their whole cruise reservation at the last minute. You have to be professional and flexible and you have to be on the ball all the time.

"It's a demanding job, but it's satisfying. People come back and say, 'I can't believe you knew exactly what I wanted. That's the best vacation I've ever had. And I'm telling all my friends.' You start getting more and more customers coming in and they ask for you by name. That feels really good. You're making a dream come true, and in a way, that's what you're doing–selling dreams."

How Mary Fallon Miller Got Started

"At the age of seven I sailed across the Atlantic on the S.S. France, and then, later, as a young woman, I accompanied my mother throughout Europe and South America. I fell in love with the glamour and excitement of travel. It gets in your blood; I have a real fascination for other cultures and languages. I realized that a career as a travel agent would allow me to pursue my dream to see more of the world."

Expert Advice

"Read *Time, Newsweek*, and your local newspaper. Try to stay in touch with the world. Listen to National Public Radio or watch the travel channel on television.

"Don't be afraid of learning the computer, study languages, and, if you have the chance, participate in a language club or take advantage of a foreign exchange program. I lived in Poland for a summer.

"Most important, learn communication skills. And, at the beginning, when you're doing some of the drudgery work, it helps to remember that down the road you will receive discounts and free travel, that you have something you are working toward. The hard work will pay off."

● ● ●

FOR MORE INFORMATION

American Society of Travel Agents
1101 King Street
Alexandria, VA 22314

Association of Retail Travel Agents
845 Sir Thomas Court, Suite 3
Harrisburg, PA 17109

Institute of Certified Travel Agents
148 Linden Street
P.O. Box 56
Wellesley, MA 02181

CHAPTER 6 Real Estate Agents, Brokers, and Appraisers

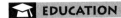
EDUCATION
H.S. Required
Other

$$$ SALARY/EARNINGS
$16,000 to $40,000

OVERVIEW

The purchase or sale of a home or investment property is not only one of the most important financial events in peoples' lives, but one of the most complex transactions as well. As a result, people generally seek the help of real estate agents, brokers, and appraisers when buying or selling real estate.

Brokers and Agents

Real estate agents and brokers have a thorough knowledge of the housing market in their community. They know which neighborhoods will best fit their clients' needs and budgets. They are familiar with local zoning and tax laws, and know where to obtain financing.

Agents and brokers also act as a medium for price negotiations between buyer and seller.

REAL ESTATE BROKERS are independent business people who, for a fee, sell real estate owned by others and rent and manage properties. In closing sales, brokers often provide buyers with information on loans to finance their purchase. They also arrange for title searches and for meetings between buyers and sellers when details of the transactions are agreed upon and the new owners take possession. A broker's knowledge, resourcefulness, and creativity in arranging financing that is most favorable to the prospective buyer often mean the difference between success and failure in closing a sale.

In some cases, agents assume the responsibilities in closing sales, but, in many areas, this is done by lawyers or lenders. Brokers also manage their own offices, supervise associate agents, advertise properties, and handle other business matters. Some combine other types of work, such as the sale of insurance or the practice of law, with their real estate business.

REAL ESTATE AGENTS generally are independent sales workers who provide their services to a licensed broker on a contract basis. In return, the broker pays the agent a portion of the commission earned from property sold through the firm by the agent. Today, relatively few agents receive salaries as employees of a broker or realty firm. Instead, most derive their income solely from commissions.

Responsibilities

Before showing properties to potential buyers, the broker or agent has an initial meeting with them to get a feeling for the type of home they would like and can afford. Then, the broker or agent takes them to see a number of homes that are likely to meet their needs and income. Because buying real estate is such an important part of the average person's life, agents may have to meet several times with a prospective buyer to discuss properties. In answering questions, agents emphasize those selling points that are likely to be most important to the buyer. To a young family looking at a house, for example, they may point out the convenient floor plan and the fact that quality schools and shopping centers are close by. To a potential investor seeking the tax advantages of owning a rental property, they may point out the proximity to the city and the ease of finding a renter. If bargaining over price becomes necessary, agents must carefully follow the seller's instructions and may have to present counter-offers in order to get the best possible price.

Once the contract has been signed by both parties, the real estate broker or agent must see to it that all special terms of the contract are met before the closing date. For example, if the seller has agreed to a home inspection or a termite and radon inspection, the agent must make sure that this is done. Also, if the seller has agreed to any repairs, the broker or agent must see to it that they have been made, otherwise the sale cannot be completed. Increasingly, brokers and agents must handle environmental problems or make sure the property they are selling meets environmental regulations. For example, they may be responsible for dealing with problems such as lead paint on the walls. While many other details are handled by loan officers, attorneys, or other persons, the agent must check to make sure that they are completed.

There is more to agents' and brokers' jobs, however, than just making a sale. Because they must have properties to sell, they spend a significant amount of time obtaining listings (owner agreements to place properties for sale with the firm). They spend much time on the telephone exploring leads gathered from various sources, including personal contacts. When listing property for sale, agents and brokers make comparisons with similar properties that have been sold recently to determine its fair market value.

Most real estate agents and brokers sell residential property. A few, usually in large firms or specialized small firms, sell commercial, industrial, agricultural, or other types of real estate. Each specialty requires knowledge of that particular type of property and clientele. Selling or leasing business property, for example, requires an understanding of leasing practices, business trends, and location needs. Agents who sell or lease industrial properties must know about transportation, utilities, and labor supply. To sell residential properties, the agent must know the location of schools, religious institutions, shopping facilities, and public transportation, and be familiar with tax rates and insurance coverage.

Agents and brokers increasingly use computers to generate lists of properties for sale, their location and description, and to identify available sources of financing.

Appraisers

Real estate transactions involve substantial financial commitments, so parties to the transactions usually seek the advice of real estate appraisers, objective experts who do not have a vested interest in the property. An appraisal is an unbiased estimate of the quality, value, and best use of a specific property. Appraisals may be used by prospective sellers to set a competitive price, by a lending institution to estimate the market value of a property as a condition for a mortgage loan, or by local governments to determine the assessed value of a property for tax purposes.

Many real estate appraisers are independent fee appraisers or work for real estate appraisal firms, while others are employees of banks, savings and loan associations, mortgage companies, and multiservice real estate companies.

During an inspection, real estate appraisers evaluate the quality of the construction, the overall condition of the property, and its functional design. They gather information on properties by taking measurements, interviewing persons familiar with the properties' history, and searching public records of sales, leases, assessments, and other transactions. They then estimate the present cost of reproducing any structures on the properties and how much the value of structures may have depreciated over time. Taking into consideration the location of the properties, current market conditions, and real estate trends or impending changes that could influence the future value of the properties, appraisers arrive at estimates of their value.

Depending on the purpose of the appraisal, they may estimate the market value of the property, the insurable value, the investment value, or other kinds of value. Appraisers must prepare formal written reports of their findings that meet the standards of the Appraisal Foundation.

Real estate appraisers often specialize in certain types of properties. Most appraise only homes, but others specialize in appraising apartment or office buildings, shopping centers, or a variety of other types of commercial, industrial, or agricultural properties.

Although real estate agents, brokers, and appraisers generally work in offices, much of their time is spent outside the office showing properties to customers, analyzing properties for sale, meeting with prospective clients, researching the state of the market, inspecting properties for appraisal, and performing a wide range of other duties. Brokers provide office space, but agents generally furnish their own automobiles.

TRAINING

Real estate agents and brokers must be licensed in every state and in the District of Columbia. All states require prospective agents to be high school graduates, be at least 18 years old, and pass a written test. The examination, which is more comprehensive for brokers than for agents, includes questions on basic real estate transactions and on laws affecting the sale of property.

Most states require candidates for the general sales license to complete at least 30 hours of classroom instruction and those seeking the broker's license to complete 90 hours of formal training in addition to a specified amount of experience in selling real estate (generally 1 to 3 years). Some states waive the experience requirements for the broker's license for applicants who have a bachelor's degree in real estate. A small but increasing number of states require that agents have 60 hours of college credit–roughly the equivalent of an associate degree.

State licenses generally must be renewed every year or two, usually without reexamination. Many states, however, require continuing education for license renewal.

Federal law requires appraisers of most types of real estate (all property being financed by a federally regulated lender) to be state certified. In some states, appraisers who are not involved with federally regulated institutions do not have to be certified. State certification requirements for appraisers must meet federal standards, but states are free to set more stringent requirements.

Formal courses, appraisal experience, and a satisfactory score on an examination are needed to be certified, but college education may be substituted for a portion of the experience requirement. Requirements for licensure vary by state but are somewhat less stringent than for certification.

Individuals enter real estate appraisal from a variety of backgrounds. Traditionally, persons enter from real estate sales, management, and finance positions. However, a growing number of people are entering appraiser jobs directly from college. College courses in real estate, finance and business administration, economics, and English are helpful. Many junior and community colleges offer two-year degrees in real estate or appraisal. Trainee appraisers usually assist experienced appraisers until they become licensed.

Persons who take real estate agent, broker, and appraiser positions are older, on average, than entrants to most other occupations. Many homemakers and retired persons are attracted to real estate sales by the flexible and part-time work schedules characteristic of this field and may enter, leave, and later reenter the occupation, depending on the strength of the real estate market, family responsibilities, or other personal circumstances. In addition to those who are entering or reentering the labor force, some transfer into real estate jobs from a wide range of occupations, including clerical and other sales jobs.

As real estate transactions have become more complex, involving complicated legal requirements, many firms have turned to college graduates to fill positions. A large number of agents, brokers, and appraisers have some college training, and the number of college graduates selling real estate has risen substantially in recent years.

However, personality traits are fully as important as academic background. Brokers look for applicants who possess a pleasant personality, honesty, and a neat appearance. Maturity, tact, and enthusiasm for the job are required in order to motivate prospective customers in this keenly competitive field. Agents also should be well-organized and detail-oriented, as well as have a good memory for names and faces and business details, such as taxes, zoning regulations, and local land-use laws.

Persons interested in beginning jobs as real estate agents often apply in their own communities, where their knowledge of local neighborhoods is an advantage. The beginner usually learns the practical aspects of the job, including the use of computers to locate or list available properties or identify sources of financing, under the direction of an experienced agent.

Many firms offer formal training programs for both beginners and experienced agents. Larger firms generally offer more extensive programs than smaller firms. Over 1,000 universities, colleges, and junior colleges offer courses in real estate. At some, a student can earn an associate or bachelor's degree with a major in real estate; several offer advanced degrees.

Many local real estate boards that are members of the National Association of Realtors sponsor courses covering the fundamentals and legal aspects of the field. Advanced courses in appraisal, mortgage financing, property development and management, and other subjects also are available through various National Association of Realtor affiliates.

Many real estate appraisers voluntarily earn professional designations that represent formal recognition of their professional competence and achievements. A number of appraiser organizations have programs that, through a combination of experience, professional education, and examinations, lead to the award of such designations. These professional designations are desirable because requirements for them are more stringent than state standards. Among the more common are various designations awarded by the Appraisal Institute and the American Society of Appraisers.

Advancement opportunities for agents often take the form of higher commission rates and more and bigger sales, both of which increase compensation. This occurs as agents gain knowledge and expertise and become more efficient in closing a greater number of transactions. Experienced agents can advance in many large firms to sales or general manager. Persons who have received their broker's license may open their own offices. Others with experience and training in estimating property value may become real estate appraisers, and people familiar with operating and maintaining rental properties may become property or real estate managers.

Agents, brokers, and appraisers who gain general experience in real estate and a thorough knowledge of business conditions and property values in their localities may enter mortgage financing or real estate investment counseling.

JOB OUTLOOK

Employment of real estate agents, brokers, and appraisers is expected to grow about as fast as the average for all occupations through the year 2005 as a result of the growing volume of sales of residential and commercial properties.

Despite this rising demand, however, the large majority of job openings will be due to replacement needs. Each year, tens of thousands of jobs will become available as workers transfer to other occupations or leave the labor force. Because turnover is high, real estate sales positions should continue to be relatively easy to obtain.

Not everyone is successful in this highly competitive field; many beginners become discouraged by their inability to get listings and to close a sufficient number of sales. Lacking financial sustenance and motivation, they subsequently leave the occupation. Well-trained, ambitious people who enjoy selling should have the best chance for success.

Employment growth in this field will stem primarily from increased demand for home purchases and rental units. Shifts in the age distribution of the population over the next decade or so will result in a large number of persons in the prime working ages (25 to 54 years old) with careers and family responsibilities. This is the most geographically mobile group in our society and the one that traditionally makes most of the home purchases. As their incomes rise, they also may be expected to invest in additional real estate.

Increasing use of technology and electronic information may increase the productivity of realtors and brokers. More and more real estate companies are equipped with computers, faxes, modems, and databases. Some real estate companies are even using computer-generated images to show houses to customers without even leaving the office. These devices enable one realtor to serve a greater number of customers. Use of this technology may eliminate some of the more marginal realtors such as those practicing real estate part time or between jobs. These workers will not be able to compete as easily with full-time realtors who have invested in this technology.

Employment of real estate agents, brokers, and appraisers is sensitive to swings in the economy. During periods of declining economic activity and tight credit, the volume of sales and the resulting demand for sales workers may decline. During these periods, the earnings of agents, brokers, and appraisers decline, and many work fewer hours or leave the occupation.

SALARIES

Commissions on sales are the main source of earnings for real estate agents and brokers. Few receive a salary.

The rate of commission varies according to the type of property and its value; the percentage paid on the sale of farm and commercial properties or unimproved land usually is higher than that paid for selling a home.

Commissions may be divided among several agents and brokers. The broker and the agent in the firm that obtained the listing generally share their part of the commission when the property is sold; the broker and the agent in the firm that made the sale also generally share their part of the commission.

Although an agent's share varies greatly from one firm to another, often it is about 50 or 60 percent of the total amount received by the firm. The agent who both lists and sells the property maximizes his or her commission.

Real estate agents, brokers, and appraisers who usually worked full time had median weekly earnings of $507 in 1992. The middle 50 percent earned between $323 and $802.

Income usually increases as an agent gains experience, but individual ability, economic conditions, and the type and location of the property also affect earnings. Sales workers who are active in community organizations and local real estate boards can broaden their contacts and increase their earnings. A beginner's earnings often are irregular because a few weeks or even months may go by without a sale. Although some brokers allow an agent a drawing account against future earnings, this practice is not usual with new employees. The beginner, therefore, should have enough money to live on for about six months or until commissions increase.

RELATED FIELDS

Selling expensive items such as homes requires maturity, tact, and a sense of responsibility. Other sales workers who find these character traits important in their work include automotive sales workers, securities and financial services sales workers, insurance agents and brokers, yacht brokers, travel agents, and manufacturers' representatives.

Other appraisers specialize in performing many types of appraisals besides real estate, including aircraft, antiques and fine arts, business valuations, and yachts.

INTERVIEW

Colleen Newshott
Real Estate Broker

Colleen Newshott has been in the real estate business for close to 30 years, first as an agent, then as an office manager, and finally as a broker and owner of her own company, Newshott Realty in Deerfield Beach, Florida. She currently has 12 agents working for her.

What the Job's Really Like

"When you work with customers in real estate, the most important thing is to learn how to listen to what their needs are. A lot of new agents might start out thinking that they'll sell their customers what *they* want, not what the customers want.

"Clients will have their dream home in mind with their Wish List, telling you everything they want, but oftentimes it's not what they can afford. So you have to go through that list and pick out the most important things to them. Is it necessary for them to have three bedrooms, for example, or will two do? Do you want one story or two? Then, at that point, I call in my mortgage broker and we go through their qualifications and see where they sit financially. It's very important to prequalify them. We can then see if they can afford a $100,000 house, for example, or more or less.

"Then you go to the computer and pull up everything that's in that price range. You pick out the very best ones in their price range and you start from the top and work your way down. It's a progression–you have to eliminate so many things.

"But, it's fun doing it. There's an excitement about it, for me as well as the clients. I put myself in the clients' place and I look at it as though I'm looking at that house for me, that it's going to be my home. By doing that, I can relate better to the clients' needs. I still get just as excited with every house I sell.

"Just yesterday I was working with a young couple and we started out looking in the $150,000 range. Then we realized we were a little out of the ballpark and started exploring the

$130,000 range. But we found a house for $130,000 that had everything they wanted, everything that had been in the $150,000 homes.

"It's so exciting and satisfying to see how thrilled they felt. 'This is my castle.' And I had a part in helping them to realize their dream.

"There are a lot of downsides to this profession, though. Lots of times you will get into a position where a deal can fall through at the last minute. For example, I always tell my clients not to go spending any money until we get through the closing, because it will change their debt ratio. The mortgage company approved their loan based on a certain credit rating. But they check the status again, a week before closing usually, sometimes even two days before closing, and if the clients have gone out and charged a lot of new furniture or whatever, it changes things. This happened recently. I advised them to be careful, I always stress this so strongly, but some people won't listen, and it killed the deal.

"You also have to be very careful when you're dealing with new clients who are strangers. Especially for women realtors. I always encourage my agents to work in pairs and to always arrange the first meeting with the client to be at the office, not at the property. This way you can get a feel for the person, get to know him a little bit. You can have that sixth sense about people. It's a good policy to follow. Then, if you have any doubts you can get someone to go with you.

"But then there are a lot of agents who feel they can disregard that policy, they trust everybody. But sometimes, you'll get men calling the office and insisting that you meet them at the house. If they refuse to come to the office, then I'll send one of the guys and give the deal to that person. As a broker, I'll still make 40 percent of the commission. For agents, though, they don't want to lose the sale completely. But if you're not sure about the client, it's better to go with another agent and then share the commission.

"Another precaution is not to take anybody in your car; you can have the clients follow you in their own car. Once at the property, after you've unlocked the front door, you should go directly to the rear exit to unlock that, just in case you need to get out quickly. That becomes ingrained in you to do that. It can be a scary business.

"Another downside is that commission sales can be very hard in dry periods. You have to have a cushion to carry you through. But if you work smart, you can make so much money in this business. With little effort you could easily bring home the equivalent of $1000 a week. But, a lot of people need to have that weekly paycheck, though, so they work a 40-hour week, then try to sell real estate part-time. But that's hard to do and you end up not making much money at it.

"By working smart I mean, following up on your clients, knowing your properties, knowing what's available, so when you do get a blind call–it's known as a floor call–you know what's out there and you can discuss things intelligently. You've got to know the market. With all my agents, we first preview every new listing.

"There are always times when you show a client 20 properties and you don't sell a thing. You can spend a lot of time, but I don't look at it as wasted time. I have increased my mental inventory, I have found out more about what's out there and I can use that information for the next call. This is working smart. You're helping the people you're working with, but you're also helping yourself.

"As far as the finances go, as a broker I get 40 percent of all commissions. The agent gets either 3 or 6 percent of the purchase price, depending upon whether he listed the property or another agent did. So, say it is a shared listing on a $100,000 home. Three percent of that comes to $3,000 and the agent keeps $1,800. Most of my 40 percent, the $1200, goes back into the office, there's a lot of overhead. The rent, the electricity, the advertising. You're lucky if you net 10 percent. But the more agents a broker has, the more money you'll make.

"Most of my agents have been with me for 20 years, and I'm always willing to sponsor new agents. It saves them money on their training course and then the state knows that they'll be working with me for at least one year when they finish.

"When I take on new agents, I always provide them with one-on-one training. From the time we get that floor call to the contracts and closing, I take them out in the field and walk them through every step, until they're comfortable doing it on their own. The best training is right on the job."

How Colleen Newshott Got Started

"First of all, I enjoy working with people and real estate provided me with an opportunity to be in a position where I could help people. Young people particularly. I have families that I'm still working with that I started out with when I first came to Florida in 1975 and opened up my business.

"Real estate is also a great opportunity to make money, and you're your own boss. I like doing things my way.

"I started out in 1967 in Ohio and went through all sorts of real estate training and classes, mostly at community colleges. It took about nine months, and I learned all about contracts, and financing and how to qualify customers, and all the other aspects of the business. Then I worked as an apprentice agent with a licensed broker for one year. I moved to Florida in 1973 and then in 1974 I got my Florida real estate license. I apprenticed again for one year, which is the requirement, then I got my broker's license and opened my own office."

Expert Advice

"When you're in good times, you have to prepare for the down times. And there will be down times. You should always set aside money to see you through. There are a lot of expenses being an agent or a broker. You've got your annual board dues, you have to handle any special advertising yourself, you have to have a nice car and dress the part. But in Florida, you can get away with dressing more casually, which is good. You also try to have a little housewarming gift for your buyers at the closing.

"This is not a week-to-week paycheck. You should know how to budget very carefully. It could be as much as three months after your first sale before you get paid.

"And make sure you enjoy dealing with people. Every person you work with is a new experience. I've been in the business many years and I've found that no two deals are alike. But you'll learn something from every deal you put together.

"For all its good points, it can be a very stressful business. If you can't handle stress, then this business wouldn't be for you."

●   ●   ●

FOR MORE INFORMATION

Details on licensing requirements for real estate agents, brokers, and appraisers are available from most local real estate and appraiser organizations or from the state real estate commission or board.

For more information about opportunities in real estate work, contact:

National Association of Realtors
777 14th St., NW
Washington, DC 20005

Information on careers and licensing and certification requirements in real estate appraising is available from:

American Society of Appraisers
P.O. Box 17265
Washington, DC 20041

Appraisal Institute
875 North Michigan Ave., Suite 2400
Chicago, IL 60611-1980

CHAPTER 7

Insurance Agents and Brokers

EDUCATION

H.S. Required

B.A. Preferred

$$$ SALARY/EARNINGS

$20,000 to $40,000

OVERVIEW

Most people have their first contact with an insurance company through an insurance agent or broker. These professionals sell individuals and businesses insurance policies that provide protection against loss. Insurance agents and brokers help individuals, families, and businesses select the right policy that best provides insurance protection for their lives and health, as well as for their automobiles, jewelry, personal valuables, furniture, household items, businesses, and other properties.

Agents and brokers prepare reports, maintain records, and, in the event of a loss, help policyholders settle insurance claims. Specialists in group policies may help an employer provide employees the opportunity to buy insurance through payroll deductions. Insurance agents may work for one insurance company or as independent agents selling for several companies.

Insurance brokers do not sell for a particular company, but place insurance policies for their clients with the company that offers the best rate and coverage.

Insurance agents sell one or more of several types of insurance: life, property/casualty, health, disability, and long-term care. Life insurance agents specialize in selling policies that pay survivors when a policyholder dies. Depending on the policyholder's circumstances, a whole-life policy also can be designed to provide retirement income, funds for the education of children, or other benefits.

Life insurance agents and brokers also are sometimes called life underwriters. Information about that occupation can be found in the *Occupational Outlook Handbook.*

Property/casualty insurance agents and brokers sell policies that protect individuals and businesses from financial loss as a result of automobile accidents, fire or theft, or other property losses. Property/casualty insurance can also cover workers' compensation, product liability, or medical malpractice. Many life and property/casualty insurance agents also sell health insurance policies covering the costs of hospital and medical care or loss of income due to illness or injury.

An increasing number of insurance agents and brokers offer comprehensive financial planning services to their clients, such as retirement planning counseling. As a result, many insurance agents and brokers are also licensed to sell mutual funds, annuities, and other securities. (Securities and financial services sales representatives are discussed in *On the Job: Real People Working in Business and Finance*, NTC Publishing.)

Because insurance sales agents obtain many new accounts through referrals, it is important that agents maintain regular contact with their clients to ensure their financial needs are being met as personal and business needs change. Developing a satisfied clientele who will recommend an agent's services to other potential customers is a key to success in this field.

About one-third of all agents and brokers are self-employed.

TRAINING

For jobs selling insurance, companies prefer college graduates, particularly those who have majored in business or economics. Some hire high school graduates with potential or proven sales ability or who have been successful in other types of work. In fact, most entrants to agent and broker jobs transfer from other occupations, so they tend to be older, on average, than entrants to many other occupations.

College training may help agents or brokers grasp more quickly the technical aspects of insurance policies and the fundamentals and procedures of selling insurance. Many colleges and universities offer courses in insurance, and some schools offer a bachelor's degree in insurance. College courses in finance, mathematics, accounting, economics, business law, government, and business administration enable insurance agents or brokers to understand how social, marketing, and economic conditions relate to the insurance industry.

It is important for insurance agents and brokers to keep current with issues concerning clients. Changes in tax laws, government benefit programs, and other state and federal regulations can affect the insurance needs of clients and how agents conduct business. Courses in psychology, sociology, and public speaking can prove useful in improving sales techniques. In addition, some basic familiarity with computers is very important. The use of computers to provide instantaneous information on a wide variety of financial products has greatly improved agents' and brokers' efficiency and enabled them to devote more time to clients.

All insurance agents and brokers must obtain a license in the states where they plan to sell insurance. In most states, licenses are issued only to applicants who complete specified courses and then pass written examinations covering insurance fundamentals and the state insurance laws. Agents and brokers who plan to sell mutual funds and other securities must also obtain a separate securities license.

New agents usually receive training at the agencies where they work and, frequently, also at the insurance company's home office. Beginners sometimes attend company-sponsored classes to prepare for examinations. Others study on their own and accompany experienced agents when they call on prospective clients.

As the diversity of financial products sold by insurance agents and brokers increases, employers are placing greater emphasis on continuing professional education. Agents and brokers can hone their practical selling skills and broaden their knowledge of insurance and other financial services and planning by taking courses at colleges and universities and attending institutes, conferences, and seminars sponsored by insurance organizations.

A number of organizations offer professional designation programs which certify expertise in specialties such as life, health, or property and casualty insurance or financial consulting. Although voluntary, professional designation assures clients and employers that an agent has a thorough understanding of the relevant specialty. Many professional societies now require agents to commit to continuing education in order to retain designation. Nearly every state has or soon will make continuing education mandatory.

Insurance agents and brokers should be enthusiastic, outgoing, self-confident, disciplined, hard working, and able to communicate effectively. They should be able to inspire customer confidence. Some companies give personality tests to prospective employees because personality attributes are important in sales work. Because they usually work without supervision, agents and brokers must be able to plan their time well and have the initiative to locate new clients.

An insurance agent who shows sales ability and leadership may become a sales manager in a local office. A few advance to agency superintendent or executive positions. However, many who have built up a good clientele prefer to remain in sales work. Some, particularly in the property/casualty field, establish their own independent agencies or brokerage firms.

JOB OUTLOOK

Employment of insurance agents and brokers is expected to grow about as fast as the average for all occupations through the year 2005. Most job openings are expected to result from the need to replace agents and brokers who leave the occupation. Many beginners find it difficult to establish a sufficiently large clientele in this highly competitive business; consequently, many eventually leave for other jobs. Opportunities should be best for ambitious people who enjoy sales work and who develop expertise in a wide range of insurance and financial services.

Future demand for agents and brokers depends on the volume of sales of insurance and other financial products. The growing number of working women should increase insurance sales. Rising incomes as well as a concern for financial security also may stimulate sales of mutual funds, variable annuities, and other financial products and services. Growing demand for long-term health care and pension benefits for retirees–an increasing proportion of the population–should spur insurance sales. Sales of property/casualty insurance should rise as more people seek coverage not only for their homes, cars, and valuables, but also for expensive, advanced technology products such as home computers.

As new businesses emerge and existing firms expand coverage, sales of commercial insurance should increase. In addition, complex types of commercial coverage, such as product liability, workers' compensation, employee benefits, and pollution liability insurance, are increasingly in demand.

Employment of agents and brokers will not keep pace with the rising level of insurance sales. Using computers, agents can access an abundance of information on potential clients, allowing them to save time and money by carefully crafting individually tailored plans. Consequently, agents will be able to handle a greater volume of sales. Many companies and agencies are diversifying their marketing techniques to include some direct mail or telephone sales, as well as other methods. These methods reduce the time agents must spend developing sales leads, allowing them to concentrate on following up on leads. In some cases, clients can purchase policies without a visit from an agent. Also, customer service representatives are increasingly assuming some sales functions, such as expanding accounts and, occasionally, generating new accounts. The trend toward multiline agents, self-insurance, and group policies also will cause employment to rise more slowly than the volume of insurance sales. In addition, large firms may increasingly hire risk managers to analyze their insurance needs and select the best policies.

Most individuals and businesses consider insurance a necessity, regardless of economic conditions. Therefore, agents are not likely to face unemployment because of a recession.

SALARIES

The median annual earnings of salaried insurance sales workers was $30,100 in 1992. The middle 50 percent earned between $20,900 and $42,200 a year.

Most independent agents are paid on a commission only basis, whereas sales workers who are employees of an agency may be paid in one of three ways: salary only, salary plus commission, or salary plus bonus.

Commissions, however, are the most common form of compensation, especially for experienced agents. The amount of the commission depends on the type and amount of insurance sold, and whether the transaction is a new policy or a renewal. Bonuses are usually awarded when agents meet their production goals or when an agency's profit goals are met. Some agents involved with financial planning receive an hourly fee for their services rather than a commission.

Agency-paid benefits to sales agent employees generally include continuing education, group insurance plans, and office space and support services. Many agencies also pay for automobile and transportation expenses, conventions and meetings, promotion and marketing expenses, and retirement plans. Independent agents working for insurance agencies receive fewer benefits, but their commissions may be higher to help them pay for promotion and marketing expenses. They are typically responsible for their own travel and automobile expenses, life insurance, and retirement plans, and receive no paid holidays or vacations. In addition, all agents are legally responsible for any mistakes that they make, and independent agents must purchase their own insurance to cover damages from their errors and omissions.

RELATED FIELDS

Other workers who sell financial products or services include real estate agents and brokers, securities and financial services sales representatives, financial advisors, estate planning specialists, and manufacturers' sales workers.

INTERVIEW
Bernice Ricciardelli
Insurance Agent

Bernice Ricciardelli works for a State Farm Insurance agent in Delray Beach, Florida. She has been in the insurance field for close to 20 years.

What the Job's Really Like

"Although I work for a State Farm agent, I am not employed by State Farm, I am employed directly by the agent. My boss sells insurance for State Farm. He has a contract with them that says he will sell insurance only for State Farm. They pay him a commission on everything he sells and he also gets a commission on everything I sell.

"My boss pays me a salary directly, about $30,000 a year. I didn't want to work on a bonus or commission basis. I prefer the security of a regular paycheck.

"I couldn't have my own contract with State Farm because I don't have a college degree. This is quite common for State Farm. Different companies have different set ups, but in order to work for State Farm, you have to have that degree. Some companies will take office personnel and make them associate agents without a bachelor's degree. Other companies aren't as strict as we are.

"Office personnel are required to be licensed by the state of Florida. We also have to sign no-compete contracts with State Farm and with my agent. State Farm can't fire us or have anything to do with our working atmosphere because I don't work directly for them.

"Besides, right now in Florida there is a long list of people waiting to become contracted State Farm agents, but State Farm isn't writing any business that they're even hiring any agents.

"This is because of Hurricane Andrew. State Farm stopped writing homeowners' and renters' insurance policies and some business policies. This is in Florida. I know Texas, California, and Hawaii are also having similar problems because of all the losses due to the bad weather. You'd have to check what's happening in other states.

"We still write auto, life, and health policies. Occasionally, we insure a boat and sometimes do a floater policy for jewelry for people who already have insurance with us.

"We can write homeowners' policies through the state of Florida, but they have such strict criteria. For example, you have to get your policy within the first 45 days of closing or leasing or else they won't write a policy either.

"Even though I have my license, I'm not allowed out of the office, and I'm not supposed to solicit business either. I run the office and do all the applications. My boss doesn't spend much time in the office so I handle pretty much everything. After all these years I know what to do and I don't have to rely on him.

"When he started with this business over 20 years ago, he had to go house to house to build up his business. So, he paid his dues and now he can afford to pay us and he earns his income by the work we do. That's something most agents can work toward. My license is the same as his, I just don't want the responsibility.

"There are just two of us, we're a small office. Some have more personnel, maybe nine or ten. People call with questions and if they want a new policy I handle it. We have people who come in and ask for quotes on different kinds of insurance.

"I interview customers and if they like the price, I go over the coverage and if they like the policy, I write it up for them. Then we service the policies. If there are problems or claims, we take the report and do all the paperwork. We go over questions.

"Sometimes we take a lot of abuse. People think we're stealing their money. They get annoyed with us because State Farm has been raising its prices. Or they might just be unhappy with the insurance business generally.

"We're on the phone a lot, maybe 70 percent of the time, and that can be frustrating. But even though the downside is the people when they're nasty, the people are the upside, too. I've been here so long I've made friends with a lot of my customers and I enjoy that. That's something you build up over the years.

"I like the job in general. I think insurance is important. I think you need good coverage. I don't like these bucket shops that don't provide their customers with adequate coverage. Life insurance is really important. If you have little children and no protection, that's not wise.

"I work 9 to 5, Monday through Friday. Sometimes there's a problem you take home with you mentally, but no paperwork. Our boss believes that we should have our free time. Other offices expect their agents or employees to put in overtime.

"It's an interesting field. Nothing is ever the same, it changes every day. Company policies and rules change and it's a continual learning experience. You have to keep up with it.

"You also have to go to continuing education classes to keep your licenses current. I have two licenses, health and life as well as property and casualty. I have to go to school for 14 hours for each license every two years. But it's boring and a waste of time and money. The program is set up for independent offices, which are completely different from State Farm. Even the lecturer knows we shouldn't have to be there, but the state and State Farm requires it."

How Bernice Ricciardelli Got Started

"I was going through a divorce and needed to get back into the workforce. The gal across the street worked for another State Farm agent. I went to work with her part time and then she quit and they gave the job to me. I worked with that agent for about three-and-a-half years then went to my current job where I've been for more than fourteen years.

"It wasn't something I'd planned, I just fell into it. I enjoy the people and the work and that's why I stayed with it."

Expert Advice

"You have to like the public and you have to know how to advise customers properly. Usually, when agents like the work, they stay in it for a long time. If they don't like it, they tend to get out of it right away.

"I'd suggest you go with an agent for a while to see what it's like and talk to several other agents and see how they feel about it. Then you can decide if the work is for you. "

● ● ●

FOR MORE INFORMATION

General occupational information about insurance agents and brokers is available from the home office of many life and casualty insurance companies. Information on state licensing requirements may be obtained from the department of insurance at any state capital.

Information about a career as a life insurance agent also is available from:

National Association of Life Underwriters
1922 F St., NW.
Washington, DC 20006

For information about insurance sales careers in independent agencies and brokerages, contact:

National Association of Professional Insurance Agents
400 N. Washington St.
Alexandria, VA 22314

For information about professional designation programs, contact:

American Society of CLU and ChFC
270 Bryn Mawr Ave.
Bryn Mawr, PA 19010-2195

Society of Certified Insurance Counselors
3630 North Hills Dr.
Austin, TX 78731

Society of Chartered Property and Casualty Underwriters
Kahler Hall
720 Providence Rd.
P.O. Box 3009
Malvern, PA 19355-0709

CHAPTER 8 Cashiers, Counter, and Rental Clerks

 **EDUCATION**
H.S. Required

$$$ SALARY/EARNINGS
Minimum wage to $13,000

OVERVIEW

Cashiers

Supermarkets, department stores, gasoline service stations, movie theaters, restaurants, and many other businesses employ cashiers to facilitate the sale of their merchandise. Most cashiers total bills, receive money, make change, fill out charge forms, and give receipts.

Although specific job duties vary by employer, cashiers are usually assigned to a register and given a drawer at the beginning of their shifts. The drawer contains a bank of money. Cashiers must count their bank to ensure it contains the correct amount of money and that there is an adequate supply of change. At the end of their shift, they once again count the drawer's contents and compare the totals with sales data. An occasional shortage of small amounts may be overlooked, but repeated shortages are grounds for dismissal in many establishments.

Cashiers traditionally have rung up customers' purchases using a cash register, manually entering the price of each product the consumer was buying. However, most establishments are now using more sophisticated equipment, such as scanners and computers. In stores with scanners, the cashier passes the product's Universal Product Code (UPC) over the scanning device, which transmits the code number to a computer. The computer identifies the item and its price. In other establishments, cashiers manually enter a code into a computer, and a description of the item and its price appear on the screen.

After entering all items and subtracting the value of any coupons or special discounts, cashiers total the bill and take payment. Depending on the type of establishment, payment may be by cash, check, charge, or increasingly, debit card. Cashiers must know the store's policies and procedures for accepting each type of payment. For checks and charges, they may have to request additional identification from the customer or call in for an authorization. When the sale is complete, cashiers issue a receipt to the customer and return the appropriate change. They may also wrap or bag the purchase.

In addition to counting the contents of their drawer at the end of their shift, cashiers usually separate charge forms, return slips, coupons, and any other non-cash items. Cashiers may also handle returns and exchanges. They must ensure that the merchandise is in good condition and determine where and when it was purchased and the type of payment used.

Cashiers may have other duties as well. In many supermarkets, for example, they weigh produce and bulk food as well as return unwanted items to the shelves. In convenience stores, cashiers may be required to know how to use a variety of machines other than cash registers, and how to furnish money orders. Operating ticket-dispensing machines and answering questions are common duties for cashiers who work at movie theaters and ticket agencies.

Counter and Rental Clerks

Counter and rental clerks perform duties similar to those of cashiers. Whether renting power tools, dropping off clothes to be dry-cleaned, or getting appliances serviced, we rely on counter and rental clerks to handle these transactions efficiently.

Although specific duties vary by establishment, counter and rental clerks are responsible for answering questions involving product availability, cost, and rental provisions. They may give other types of advice as well. Counter and rental clerks also take orders, calculate fees, receive payments, and accept returns. (Retail sales workers, occupations with similar duties, are discussed in Chapter 1.)

Regardless of where they work, counter and rental clerks must be knowledgeable about the company's services, policies, and procedures. For example, in the car rental industry, they inform customers about the features of the different types of automobiles available and their daily and weekly rental costs, ensure that customers meet age or other requirements, and indicate when and in what condition the car must be returned. In dry-cleaning establishments, counter clerks inform customers when items will be ready. In other establishments, counter and rental clerks use their special knowledge to give advice on a wide variety of products and services ranging from hydraulic tools to shoe repair.

When taking orders counter and rental clerks use various types of equipment. In some establishments, they write out tickets and order forms. However, computers and bar code scanners are quickly becoming the norm. Most computer systems are user friendly and usually require very little data entry. Scanners read the product code and display a description of the item on a computer screen. Clerks must ensure, however, that the data on the screen matches the actual product.

More than one-half of all cashiers are on part-time schedules. Four out of ten counter and rental clerks also work part-time.

TRAINING

Cashier jobs tend to be entry-level positions requiring little or no previous work experience. Although there are no specific educational requirements, employers filling full-time jobs often prefer applicants with a high school diploma.

Nearly all cashiers are trained on the job. In small firms, beginners are often trained by an experienced worker. The first day is usually spent observing the operation and becoming familiar with the store's equipment, policies, and procedures. After this, trainees are assigned to a register–frequently under the supervision of a more experienced worker. In larger firms, before being placed at a cash register, trainees first spend several days in classes. Topics typically covered include a description of the industry and the company, instruction on the store's policies, procedures, and equipment operation, and security.

Training for experienced workers is not common except when new equipment is introduced or when procedures change. In these cases, training is given on the job by the employer or a representative of the equipment manufacturer.

People who want to become cashiers should be able to do repetitious work accurately. They also need basic arithmetic skills, good manual dexterity and, because they deal constantly with the public, cashiers should be neat in appearance and be able to deal tactfully and pleasantly with customers. Good oral and written communication skills are essential for counter and rental clerks.

In addition, some firms seek people who have operated specialized equipment or who have business experience, such as typing, selling, or handling money.

Advancement opportunities vary. Depending on the size of the company, jobs as cashiers or counter and rental clerks can lead to more responsible positions. For those working part time, promotion may be to a full-time position. Others advance to head cashier, cash office clerk, or into assistant manager positions.

In certain industries, such as equipment repair, counter and rental jobs may be an additional or alternate source of income for workers who are unemployed or entering semi-retirement. For example, a retired mechanic could prove invaluable at a tool rental center because of his or her relevant knowledge.

JOB OUTLOOK

Employment of cashiers is expected to increase about as fast as the average for all occupations through the year 2005 due to expanding demand for goods and services by a growing population.

Employment for counter and rental clerks is expected to increase faster than the average for all occupations through the year 2005 due to anticipated employment growth in the industries where they are concentrated–laundries and dry cleaners, equipment rental and leasing, automotive rentals, and amusement and recreation services.

Although growth will account for numerous openings, most jobs will result from the need to replace experienced workers who transfer to other occupations or leave the labor force. As in the past, replacement needs will create a significant number of job openings, for the occupation is large and turnover is much higher than average. Opportunities for part-time work are expected to continue to be excellent.

Workers under the age of 25 traditionally have filled many of the openings in these occupations. This age group shrank in numbers during the decade of the 1980s, and although it will rebound during the 1990s, it will not attain its 1992 share of the workforce until about 2005. To attract and retain workers, employers may offer higher wages, additional benefits, and flexible schedules. Recruitment efforts also may be directed toward nontraditional groups such as retired or disabled persons.

SALARIES

Cashiers, counter, and rental clerks have earnings ranging from the minimum wage to several times that amount. Wages tend to be higher in areas where there is intense competition for workers. In addition to their wages, some counter and rental clerks receive commissions based on the number of contracts they complete or services they sell.

In 1992, median weekly earnings for full-time cashiers were about $219. Retail counter clerks earned a median weekly income of $252 in 1992.

Benefits for full-time workers tend to be better than for those working part time. Workers often receive health and life insurance and paid vacations. In addition, those working in retail establishments often receive discounts on purchases and those in restaurants may receive free or low-cost meals. Many companies offer discounts to both full- and part-time employees on the services they provide.

RELATED FIELDS

Other workers with similar duties include food counter clerks, bank tellers, postal service clerks, and retail sales clerks.

INTERVIEW
Brent Van Ham
Cashier

Brent Van Ham has worked for J. D. Streett Mobil Service Station in Carbondale, Illinois for three years while attending Southern Illinois University. He will graduate with a bachelor's degree in psychology. He plans to go on to become a registered nurse.

What the Job's Really Like

"The job is basically selling gas, cigarettes, snack food, and lottery tickets. The station is on a main road and it's the busiest station in town. It's a self-service station with a minimart inside. We have eight pumps in front and four on the side. Three walls of the store are covered with cigarettes, about 4,000 cartons. If you're there when an order comes in you stock the shelves. I handle the register, credit card authorizations, and the Lotto machine, which is a separate register.

"We accept checks, but it's up to the clerk to decide whether to accept a check from someone or not. I go by gut instinct and what's on the check. We're supposed to look at the check number to judge the newness of the account and take only checks that are numbered 500 and above. But anyone can throw away the first 500 and order a new set of checks. The checks should be local and have all the information and driver's license number and such. A couple of times a check bounced and I paid for them. We're not responsible by law to pay for them, but I pay for them when they're really stupid mistakes I've made. Like when the number was under 500 and someone was using a friend's check and I took it as a favor. I felt bad; we're supposed to eye them. If it's someone just passing through and they're buying five cartons of cigarettes with a check numbered 200, you kind of wonder about it.

"We also handle the deposits. You spend the last half hour of every shift taking care of the math. You take a receipt from the beginning of the shift and the end of the shift and come up with the difference. Then you match that to how much money you have. The boss makes a daily deposit except on Sunday. The tape runs from Saturday all the way to Monday.

"There are about 11 cashiers on the crew. About half are students, the rest work full time. Except for the midnight shift we have two people on at a time. We have two registers. It's very busy all day, and even though we're supposed to be enthusiastic about that, sometimes it's incredibly busy. We get a line out to the highway and the store full of people and there's only two cashiers. Yesterday, the Lotto was up to $31 million and I sold a thousand tickets in eight hours. That's not counting the gas or cigarette sales. We're supposed to be held accountable for anything that's missing. People do try to steal, and with so much going on it's hard to watch everyone.

"And then you have to deal with rude people all the time. Being rude is a recurrent theme and after a day of that you can feel pretty worn down.

"I enjoy the give and take, though. It's amazing. I've never met so many different kinds of people in my life. Some people think this kind of work would be dull, but it's really very interesting. Every type of person that exists goes to a gas station, from farmers to sophisticated university professors. We also get a lot of strange ones. For example, we have a person who comes in for a dollar of gas every day. Someone else comes in twice a day for a dollar of gas each time. He never fills up the tank. I haven't asked him why; we're all a little scared of him.

"The midnight shift is pure craziness. We get the people who are really out there; they wander around when the sun goes down. We get the drunks, too, but we also get a lot of police officers.

"I haven't had too many problems on the midnight shift; we've never been held up. I think it's because we're in a very accessible area. And I'm very nice to the police officers so they come by and chat a lot. But I have run into some situations–people coming behind the counter looking to start a fight. I keep a baseball bat back there.

"If you're working the night shift you basically have another role to play. In addition to cashier, you're also a security guard.

"The store is open 24 hours a day, 7 days a week. We're even open on Christmas. I work anywhere from 17 hours a week to putting in overtime, over 40 hours, and rotate through all three shifts. We have a morning shift from 6 to 2, and then there's 2 to 10 at night, then 10 to 6. We know our schedule a week in advance. My boss knows I take classes so he never schedules me on top of them. Usually I work the second shift during the week and the midnight shift on weekends.

"I also cover sometimes for my coworkers. We can trade shifts if something comes up. Basically the hours are flexible, and that's the main perk. I get to call the shots week to week.

"I'm paid hourly–$5.25 an hour. There are no other real benefits such as health insurance, but they take an average of my hours over a year and give me either a check for an average week or they give me the time off. Last year my average was 30 hours–I took the check."

How Brent Van Ham Got Started

"I had a roommate doing the same work. I was looking for a job and he took me to meet his boss. I walked in with the application and got hired within five minutes. I started that same day.

"They put me on the midnight shift for two days to train me, then I was set on my own. I worked those shifts with the midnight person who was quitting. The training covered all the duties and especially running the cash register. I'm computer literate but I never really operated a cash register before."

Expert Advice

"I think anyone who has the intelligence to do this job successfully should be looking at it as a step. I don't think anyone should be locked into this. If you can figure out a register and come out on the money and deal with people, you should be able to move up into other types of work.

"I could have asserted myself more and I could have been assistant manager by now, but I wouldn't want to. I'm not going to stay. Even if I can't get a job in my field after I graduate I still would leave this job. I look at it as a step I had to take.

"This job is like a double-sided coin. You have to be wary of people–there's always someone looking to pull a scam–but on the other hand, you can really make a change with people. Most people who come in look at the cashier as a nonperson and they go about their business and talk to themselves and sometimes if a person is in a bad mood I can snap them out of it just by being nice. But it can work the other way and their moods can rub off on you.

"This is not a brain dead job. All the people who work here and stay here are pretty smart. It's a lot of responsibility. There's a lot of money a shift moving through that store. Plus all the people that come with it."

•   •   •

FOR MORE INFORMATION

For information about employment opportunities as a cashier, contact:

National Association of Convenience Stores
1605 King St.
Alexandria, VA 22314-2792

Service Station Dealers of America
801 N. Fairfax St., Suite 109
Alexandria, VA 22314

United Food and Commercial Workers Union
1775 K St., NW
Washington, DC 20006-1502

For more information about opportunities as counter and rental clerks contact:

Association of Progressive Rental Organizations
6300 Bridgepoint Parkway
Austin, TX 78730

CHAPTER 9 Marketing Managers

🎓 **EDUCATION**
B.A. Required
M.A. Preferred

$$$ **SALARY/EARNINGS**
$21,000 to $75,000+

OVERVIEW

The fundamental objective of any firm is to market its products or services profitably. In small firms, all marketing responsibilities may be assumed by the owner or chief executive officer. In large firms, which may offer numerous products and services nationally or even worldwide, experienced marketing, advertising, and public relations managers coordinate these and related activities.

Marketing Managers

The executive vice president for marketing in large firms directs the overall marketing policy including market research, marketing strategy, sales, advertising, promotion, pricing, product development, and public relations activities. These activities are supervised by middle and supervisory managers who oversee staffs of professionals and technicians.

Marketing managers develop the firm's detailed marketing strategy. With the help of subordinates, including product development managers and market research managers, they determine the demand for products and services offered by the firm and its competitors and identify potential consumers such as business firms, wholesalers, retailers, government, or the general public. Mass markets are further categorized according to various factors such as region, age, income, and lifestyle.

Marketing managers develop pricing strategy with an eye toward maximizing the firm's share of the market and its profits while ensuring that the firm's customers are satisfied. In collaboration with sales, product development, and other managers, they monitor trends that indicate the need for new products and services and oversee product development.

Marketing managers work with advertising and promotion managers to best promote the firm's products and services and to attract potential users.

Sales Managers

Sales managers direct the firm's sales program. They assign sales territories and goals and establish training programs for their sales representatives. Managers advise their sales representatives on ways to improve their sales performance. In large, multi-product firms, they oversee regional and local sales managers and their staffs. Sales managers maintain contact with dealers and distributors. They analyze sales statistics gathered by their staffs to determine sales potential and inventory requirements and monitor the preferences of customers. Such information is vital to develop products and maximize profits.

Advertising Managers

Except in the largest firms, advertising and promotion staffs are generally small and serve as a liaison between the firm and the advertising or promotion agency to which many advertising or promotional functions are contracted out.

Advertising managers oversee the account services, creative services, and media services departments. The account services department is managed by account executives, who assess the need for advertising and, in advertising agencies, maintain the accounts of clients.

The creative services department develops the subject matter and presentation of advertising. This department is supervised by a creative director, who oversees the copy chief and art director and their staffs. The media services department is supervised by the media director, who oversees planning groups that select the communication media–for example, radio, television, newspapers, magazines, or outdoor signs to disseminate the advertising.

Promotion Managers

Promotion managers supervise staffs of promotion specialists. They direct promotion programs combining advertising with purchase incentives to increase sales of products or services. In an effort to establish closer contact with purchasers-dealers distributors, or consumers–promotion programs may involve direct mail, telemarketing, television or radio advertising, catalogs, exhibits, inserts in newspapers, in-store displays and product endorsements, and special events. Purchase incentives may include discounts, samples, gifts, rebates, coupons, sweepstakes, and contests.

Public Relations Managers

Public relations managers supervise public relations specialists. These managers direct publicity programs to a targeted public. They use any necessary communication media in their effort to maintain the support of the specific group upon whom their organization's success depends, such as consumers, stockholders, or the general public. For example, public relations managers may clarify or justify the firm's point of view on health or environmental issues to community or special interest groups. They may evaluate advertising and promotion programs for compatibility with public relations efforts.

Public relations managers, in effect, serve as the eyes and ears of top management. They observe social, economic, and political trends that might ultimately have an effect upon the firm, and make recommendations to enhance the firm's public image in view of those trends. Public relations managers may confer with labor relations managers to produce internal company communications such as news about employee-management relations, and with financial managers to produce company reports. They may assist company executives in drafting speeches, arranging interviews, and other forms of public contact; oversee company archives; and respond to information requests. In addition, public relations managers may handle special events such as sponsorship of races, parties introducing new products, or other activities the firm supports in order to gain public attention through the press without advertising directly.

Marketing, advertising, and public relations managers are provided with offices close to top managers. Long hours, including evenings and weekends, are common. Working under pressure is unavoidable as schedules change, problems arise, and deadlines and goals must be met.

Marketing, advertising, and public relations managers meet frequently with other managers; some meet with the public and government officials.

Substantial travel may be involved. For example, attendance at meetings sponsored by associations or industries is often mandatory. Sales managers travel to national, regional, and local offices and to various dealers and distributors. Advertising and promotion managers may travel to meet with clients or representatives of communications media. Public relations managers may travel to meet with special interest groups or government officials. Job transfers between headquarters and regional offices are common–particularly among sales managers–and may disrupt family life.

Marketing, advertising, and public relations managers are found in virtually every industry. Industries employing them in significant numbers include motor vehicle dealers; printing and publishing firms; advertising agencies; department stores; computer and data processing services firms; and management and public relations firms.

TRAINING

A wide range of educational backgrounds are suitable for entry into marketing, advertising, and public relations managerial jobs, but many employers prefer a broad liberal arts background. A bachelor's degree in sociology, psychology, literature, or philosophy, among other subjects, is acceptable. However, requirements vary depending upon the particular job.

For marketing, sales, and promotion management positions, some employers prefer a bachelor's or master's degree in business administration with an emphasis on marketing. Courses in business law, economics, accounting, finance, mathematics, and statistics are also highly recommended.

In highly technical industries, such as computer and electronics manufacturing, a bachelor's degree in engineering or science combined with a master's degree in business administration may be preferred.

For advertising management positions, some employers prefer a bachelor's degree in advertising or journalism. A course of study should include courses in marketing, consumer behavior, market research, sales, communications methods and technology, and visual arts–for example, art history and photography.

For public relations management positions, some employers prefer a bachelor's or master's degree in public relations or journalism. The individual's curriculum should include courses in advertising, business administration, public affairs, political science, and creative and technical writing. For all these specialties, courses in management and completion of an internship while in school are highly recommended. Familiarity with computerized word processing and database applications also are important for many marketing, advertising, and public relations management positions.

Most marketing, advertising, and public relations management positions are filled by promoting experienced staff or related professional or technical personnel such as sales representatives, purchasing agents, buyers, product or brand specialists, advertising specialists, promotion specialists, and public relations specialists.

In small firms, where the number of positions is limited, advancement to a management position may come slowly. In large firms, promotion may occur more quickly.

Although experience, ability, and leadership are emphasized for promotion, advancement may be accelerated by participation in management training programs conducted by many large firms. Many firms also provide their employees with continuing education opportunities, either in-house or at local colleges and universities, and encourage employee participation in seminars and conferences, often provided by professional societies. Often in collaboration with colleges and universities, numerous marketing and related associations sponsor national or local management training programs. Courses include brand and product management, international marketing, sales management evaluation, telemarketing and direct sales, promotion, marketing communication, market research, organizational communication, and data processing systems procedures and management. Many firms pay all or part of the cost for those who successfully complete courses.

Some associations (listed at the end of this chapter) offer certification programs for marketing, advertising, and public relations managers. Certification is a sign of competence and achievement in this field that is particularly important in a competitive job market. While relatively few marketing, advertising, and public relations managers currently are certified, the number of managers who seek certification is expected to grow. For example, Sales and Marketing Executives International offers a management certification program based on education and job performance. The Public Relations Society of America offers an accreditation program for public relations practitioners based on years of experience and an examination. The American Marketing Association is developing a certification program for marketing managers.

Persons interested in becoming marketing, advertising, and public relations managers should be mature, creative, highly motivated, resistant to stress, and flexible, yet decisive. The ability to communicate persuasively, both orally and in writing, with other managers, staff, and the public is vital.

Marketing, advertising, and public relations managers also need tact, good judgment, and exceptional ability to establish and maintain effective personal relationships with supervisory and professional staff members and client firms.

Because of the importance and high visibility of their jobs, marketing, advertising, and public relations managers often are prime candidates for advancement. Well-trained, experienced, successful managers may be promoted to higher positions in their own or other firms. Some become top executives. Managers with extensive experience and sufficient capital may open their own businesses.

JOB OUTLOOK

Employment of marketing, advertising, and public relations managers is expected to increase faster than the average for all occupations through the year 2005. Increasingly intense domestic and global competition in products and services offered to consumers should require greater marketing, promotional, and public relations efforts.

Management and public relations firms may experience particularly rapid growth as businesses increasingly hire contractors for these services rather than support additional full-time staff.

In addition to faster-than-average growth, many job openings will occur each year as a result of managers moving into top management positions, transferring to other jobs, or leaving the labor force. However, many of these highly coveted jobs will be sought by other managers or highly experienced professional and technical personnel, resulting in substantial job competition.

College graduates with extensive experience, a high level of creativity, and strong communication skills should have the best job opportunities.

Projected employment growth varies by industry. For example, employment of marketing, advertising, and public relations managers is expected to grow much faster than average in most business services industries, such as computer and data processing, and management and public relations firms, while average growth is projected in manufacturing industries overall.

SALARIES

According to a College Placement Council survey, starting salary offers to marketing majors graduating in 1993 averaged about $24,000; advertising majors, about $21,000.

The median annual salary of marketing, advertising, and public relations managers was $41,000 in 1992. The lowest 10 percent earned $22,000 or less, while the top 10 percent earned $79,000 or more.

Many earn bonuses equal to 10 percent or more of their salaries. Surveys show that salary levels vary substantially depending upon the level of managerial responsibility, length of service, education, and the employer's size, location, and industry.

For example, manufacturing firms generally pay marketing, advertising, and public relations managers higher salaries than nonmanufacturing firms. For sales managers, the size of their sales territory is another important factor.

According to a 1992 survey by Abbot, Langer and Associates, of Crete, Illinois, annual incomes for sales/marketing managers varied greatly from under $25,000 to over $250,000, depending on the manager's level of education, experience, industry, and the number of employees he or she supervises.

The median annual income was as follows:

Advertising managers–$45,000

Product/brand managers–$54,000

Market research managers–$55,000

Regional sales managers–$64,000

Chief marketing executives–$67,000

RELATED FIELDS

Marketing, product, advertising, promotions, and public relations managers direct the sale of products and services offered by their firms and the communication of information about their firms' activities. Other personnel involved in this area include art directors, commercial and graphic artists, copy chiefs, copywriters, editors, lobbyists, marketing research analysts, public relations specialists, promotion specialists, sales representatives, and technical writers.

INTERVIEW

Chris Fuller
General Manager, Marketing and Sales, Food Services

Chris Fuller worked in food services for more than 30 years, working his way up through a variety of responsible positions. He worked at Colgate Palmolive, Pepsi Cola, and Thomas J. Lipton and retired in 1988.

What the Job's Really Like

"Food service is a secondary business within the framework of a retail business in most food companies–General Foods, or Nabisco, or Procter & Gamble, for example. Food service is usually a much smaller part of their business and normally a less profitable part of the business.

"The purpose of the food service industry, at least at Thomas J. Lipton, was to sell company products, such as tea bags, and try and get them exposed into restaurants and cafeterias–wherever food was sold throughout the United States. The retail end deals with supermarkets and smaller Mom-and-Pop stores. Food service is designed to sell products to restaurants.

"There are several functions in a food service business. One is to take the products that a retail business is selling and get them designed in the right sizes and the right types of packages to sell to restaurants. You don't necessarily sell the same product to a restaurant that you would to a consumer through a food store.

"You have to take the entire line of products you want to sell to restaurants and have them redesigned for the restaurant trade. When I was there, the major product happened to be tea bags. A tea bag that you sell to a consumer is for one cup of tea. The tea bag you'd sell to a restaurant might be for a whole jug of tea.

"The taste could be slightly different as well. For example, you may sell a very spicy product, but the restaurant doesn't want a spicy product; their clientele prefers milder tastes. Sometimes you can accommodate them, sometimes you can't, depending on how many other restaurants are in the same boat.

"Another function is marketing. Marketing is pricing, packaging, and the development of the particular product you're going to advertise, promote, and sell. You advertise in the trade journals to let customers know you're going to be offering a particular product.

"Marketing also includes sales. We worked as part of a team. We had a finance person, for example, who would tell us if we were making money or not or what kind of prices we needed in order to profit on something. This position often holds a profit responsibility. If he spends too much money, the business will lose money, and he's the guy who will go out the door.

"The sales guys, although responsible for sales volume and reaching a quota every week, do not have any profit responsibility, and they are always asking for lower prices, more advertising, and more promotion. The marketing guy says 'You can't have that much, because if we spend that much and price the product 10 cents a case less, we're going to lose money.' Marketing and sales are often at odds with each other. At budget time there is always a battle.

"I had many businesses I was responsible for. My particular job encompassed the Good Humor business and some other odds and ends. The ice cream business is enormous and very important within Lipton. They also had a little Mideast business called Sahadi and they sold fruit rolls and other products to restaurants in areas where you had a high concentration of Middle Eastern people. Lipton also has a dry soup business, Wishbone salad dressing, and they have noodles-and-sauce and rice-and-sauce businesses. Sometimes we could get that sold through restaurants if they didn't want to make that product themselves. Most restaurants like to make their own pasta though, but some don't.

"I had a person I supervised who managed the day to day of the food service end and his job was to decide what pricing promotions and advertising were needed that month to sell the product. He also decided how many salespeople he needed, what kind of training they should have, where they should be stationed, which accounts those salesmen would call on, and how much time they could give to each account.

"Food service salespeople cover a lot more territory than the retail sales end. The volume is generally lower, so you can't afford to have too many salespeople.

"There's a lot of automobile travel and a very tough schedule. Sometimes the accounts will see you when you want to see them, sometimes you have to wait and see them another day and here you are, having traveled 300 miles. So what are you going to do if you don't have it planned to see other accounts in that area? There's a lot of planning and time away from home. It affects family life very negatively.

"The sales manager has to go out and see his sales reps because they can't afford to take the time to come to you and lose sales. So, the sales manager is out in the field with his personnel too, making calls and making sure the reps are using the right techniques and handling each situation the way it should be handled in order to get the maximum sales volume.

"A step up from that, in marketing, your traveling would be a lot less. The sales manager would normally report to the vice president of marketing. Sales is part of the marketing mix.

"Although marketing is a step up, there's a downside to it. If they're not making the expected profit, they can lose their jobs. They have the same sales volume responsibility that the sales people have because the sales people report to them.

"They make an agreement with sales–they say for example, okay, we're going to sell 100 units of X to, say, Denny's. Now say they only sell 90 units. The sales guy has the first responsibility, and the marketing person does too. He had agreed that that was what could be sold with the certain advertising, price, and quality of the product. But he missed it so he's also on the line.

"It's extraordinarily time-consuming in this business, it never ends. No marketing job in today's environment is nine to five. There is always competition.

"The upside is that most successful salespeople like their job. You have to like it. If you don't like walking in and talking to people every day, this job isn't for you.

"There's a lot of shmoozing that goes on. You get to know the purchasing person and if you've been calling on him for a number of years, theoretically, you'd better get to know who his wife is and who the kids are and when their birthdays are and take him out to dinner. You're not giving expensive presents–those are out–but little courtesies are okay.

"Money is no better than it is in retail. I wouldn't say that the money is terrific. It's hard work, you're not going to end up being wealthy. But you get a good pension plan and you get bonuses.

"To run a sales organization you have to base it on who does what. There are a lot of incentives. Trips, prizes, and cash.

"When you're selling food, you're selling the brand name or a recipe. You're not selling what it can do–you're selling recognition. You might cook up a batch of macaroni and cheese for the purchaser to sample, but it's not the same as selling a computer or a car. You don't have to know how to cook. So you say, 'I don't know how to cook, but the directions here are so simple even I can do this. Just give me a pot and water and I'll show you.' If you're selling a car, you have to know all the things that that car has, the features it has. It's much more complex. Food service is much simpler in some ways."

How Chris Fuller Got Started

"What attracted me to this field was that it was kind of glamorous. You had a lot of advertising and promotion. Product managers made good money, the businesses were stable and you didn't have the big hiring and firing problems we have in the 90s. You could stay with a company for a long time. They had good programs and they were well respected in the business community all around the United States.

"I got my B.A. in economics and my M.B.A., both at Dartmouth College. That was back in 1953. I've been in this business for 30 years. I started with Colgate Palmolive in 1956. They weren't a food business, but they were analogous to it; they were in the household products business, which sold products through the same channels as the food companies. They ended up in the same stores.

"At General Foods I was manager of marketing analysis and then became a product manager in the frozen potato business. At Pepsi Cola I was vice president of finance and president of Metrop Bottling Company, which sold Pepsi through company-owned franchises in the United States.

"I went to work for Thomas J. Lipton in 1977 and had never been in food service before. I was senior vice president of operations and finance there, then became senior vice president of general management. That was a marketing job, where I managed a group of businesses including the food service end."

Expert Advice

"The most important thing is that you don't mind traveling and that you like to meet people and talk to people every day. You have to be able to follow directions. You're going to have a regional manager or a division manager over you and they will be giving you directions and you will have to follow those directions explicitly.

"What you do every day is tracked–where you have been, who you have seen, and what you have sold. Every day. You are in a fishbowl. Every salesperson in the United States has got his working life on a computer somewhere.

"You need to be a gregarious person, and you have to be thick-skinned and able to take criticism. You can get a lot of complaints from a customer. A shipment didn't come in on time. Or he thinks he was shorted or the macaroni and cheese didn't taste the same as the batch you cooked up for him that day. Are you sure it's the same product? All that kind of thing. There's constant haranguing. The purchasing agent you're dealing with has been criticized by his boss and the first guy that's going to walk through that door–you–is going to get it.

"If you go into food service, in order to advance you might want to move over to the retail side at a later date, selling to supermarkets.

"Your eventual aim is to go up the ladder in sales and then go into marketing. A lot of people from sales go into marketing. You need to start young, when you're in your twenties, then move over to marketing in your early thirties. If you don't move to marketing in your early thirties, it will be too late and you'll get stuck in sales. There's a corporate system you have to learn and follow.

"But it's a good career. It's a stable business. The companies that are in it are solid. They're not fly-by-night. For the most part, they're not going to go out of business.

"You have to get up and do something every day; you can't rest on your laurels. If you like people and competition, you'll be fine."

INTERVIEW

Kevin Whelan
Marketing/Product Manager

Kevin Whelan has had a long, successful career in marketing. He has been with Hill-Rom, a capital equipment manufacturer based in South Carolina, since 1995. He earned his M.B.A. in 1982 from Georgia State University in·Atlanta.

What the Job's Really Like

"We manufacture, distribute, and service health care sleeping surfaces. This is more than just hospital beds. The term 'health care' includes long-term care and home care as well as hospitals. 'Sleeping surfaces' covers more than just beds. For example, there are sleeping surfaces that are used to heal skin ulcers.

"In contrast to sales–a lot of people think that marketing and sales are the same thing–a salesman tries to get rid of what he has. A marketer tries to get what he can get rid of. That was a corrupted quote by Ted Levitt, a marketing professor at Harvard.

He said it in terms of sales companies versus marketing companies. But what the marketer does is start at the beginning of the cycle and look at the customer and say, 'Gee, I wonder what they need.' Having determined what the market needs, you then take a look at your company and try to determine if this is something you can produce for the customer. Do we know how to produce it and can we make money doing it?

"At that point we start interfacing with the product development people, who might be in some industries, scientists–in my industry, it's engineers. We form a team of people–myself, the vice president of marketing, marketing researchers, engineers, advertisers, a financial advisor, and eventually salespeople–that say, 'This is something our customers really want, what can we do to meet their needs?' This is the process of idea generation. The ideas might come from talking to the customers, something we saw in a magazine, or by just being out in the marketplace.

"It's a lot of pleading and cajoling and trying to convince others. And when you're trying to find out what the customers need, there's a whole group of skills that revolves around what we call market research. You might set up focus groups, bringing a group of customers together and talking to them, finding out what isn't working in their present environment. And that would bubble forth a need.

"After you do that, you want to quantify that need in the marketplace. Maybe 30 people have told you they need a particular device, but I'm not going to build that product for 30 people. I want to make sure there are enough people out there who are willing to buy such a thing. You do another set of research–this I coordinate with a researcher.

"Concept development is the next step in the process. This is where you develop a word or paragraph that describes the device. You take that to engineers who will develop a prototype. In our case, they'll make a bed.

"You then take this bed to the marketplace. This is called the alpha site test. It gets shipped to three or four nursing homes or other health care facilities and often I get on a plane and meet up with it at the end destination. You don't put anybody on this bed, it's not necessarily safe at this point; you just show it to customers–in our case that would most likely be the nurses–and ask them to evaluate it.

"You go into a little circle then of building and taking it out, building and taking it out. Each time you do that, you learn something new. We're trying to improve the product based on the suggestions we get.

"Once you are 95 percent sure this is the product you want, you take it to one big final test that's called the beta site test. Here you have a patient use the bed. After you deliver the product you leave and see if the product will work without your standing there. Later you go back and interview the nurses to see if they are happy with it. The beta site test gives you a go, no go.

"Concurrently with this you put the bed through other testing–safety checks, for example, to make sure it meets FDA guidelines. We also test for claims. At some point in the future I might want to be able to say, 'If you buy this bed, you will get great healing of skin sores.' I need to be able to document that claim.

"If it's a go, the engineers start figuring out how to mass produce it and I figure out how we can make money on it. For that I have to look at the cost and how much people are willing to pay for it. One of the big misconceptions in this business is that you take the cost and add something to it. Price is not determined that way; it's determined by what people are willing to pay. Once I have done that, I take it to the vice president of marketing for approval.

"Then we start making them and I go into the promotion planning stage. Now that I have a product I have to find a way of getting the word out. I'll make brochures and do the advertising. This is all part of my job. I also come up with ways to teach salespeople what to say about it. At the same time I'm crunching a lot of numbers, looking to see how fast the product will be made, how fast we can get out to the field, how many will be bought and what our projection is for making money.

"Once I'm able to set a date for introducing this product, we hold big sales meetings and tell the reps how to sell it, why they should sell it and send them loose.

"Then I monitor the product to see if it's meeting its sale projections. If I'm not making those numbers, my boss, the vice president of marketing, wants to know why and what I'm going to do about it. If I am making the numbers or doing better, he wants to know why, and why I'm not selling more. There's no winning in this business.

"Then I'm still following up with customers–is it still meeting their needs and if not, what changes do we have to make? I also follow up with the salespeople, what else they need to sell the product. And with the engineers–is the price right, how can we manufacture this and get the cost down?

"In a typical day, week, or month, you're constantly pushing every bit and piece of this process along–no two days are alike. The process takes anywhere from a year to five years.

"I put in probably about 50 hours a week, basically Monday through Friday, eight to six. There's also travel involved, maybe 25 percent of my time is traveling.

"I don't choose to make it a stressful job, but it could be stressful for some people, and there are stressful times. If we're introducing a product that's not going well, and sales are plummeting and we can't figure out why, it can be very stressful. In a long-term sense, my job is on the line. If sales are down on any given day, then I wouldn't be fired, but if I can't meet our profit goals over a one- to two-year period, I'd be replaced.

"What I like most is the number of different things I get to do. My job is to influence a lot of different people and the best way to do that is talk in their language. I have to be able to talk accounting to accountants, advertising to advertisers, patient care to nurses, sales techniques to the sales staff, engineering to our engineers, business management to the vice president of my company. No two conversations are alike.

"I'm paid a salary and a bonus based on the performance of the products I'm managing. The salary range for people in my type of job is $70,000 to $90,000 a year including the bonus.

"The biggest downside is that I support people–the salespeople–who are making more money than I am. A lot more money. But for me, marketing is more fun than sales."

How Kevin Whelan Got Started

"I went to Spring Hill College in Mobile, Alabama and graduated with a B.A. in history in 1978. I was then an army officer for four years. In 1982, I left the army, and looked for a job where I could be involved in activities that I'd be able to measure the results of my actions. I wanted to be involved in some sort of free enterprise business.

"I went to work for a company called American Hospital Supply as a logistics specialist. That had been my specialty in the army. Logistics is the movement of materials through distribution to some end point. In the case of American Hospital Supply, a hospital customer.

"I was there two years and in my second year I was approached to consider going into sales at the same company. I sold a variety of hospital supplies for one year with them. After one year that company was reorganizing and I was part of a reduction in their force. In other words, I was canned.

"I enjoyed the job, but I did it very poorly. My first foray into it was a disaster. I never asked people to buy anything. I would call on a hospital and show them my products. I'd ask them if they liked the products, if they liked my company, and if they liked me. And they'd always answer yes, but I never asked for the order. So getting laid off was not a surprise. I was losing money for them.

"The one attribute I did have was that I had strong relationships with customers. One of my customers was approached by another of her sales reps who worked for Kimberly-Clark and asked if she knew anyone who might be interested in selling for them in the Baltimore area. I had been in Richmond, Virginia at the time.

"She gave my name and I was hired by them. I was with them a total of ten years. The first five years were in sales and I sold in three different territories, Baltimore, Pittsburgh, and Columbus, Ohio. Kimberly-Clark gave me the training I needed. They told me to ask for the order.

"After five years I was approached by the sales manager and asked if I would consider a job in product management. The rest is history. I had gone through the various stepping stones in sales–I was a senior sales rep involved with training–and I was also taking some business courses at Ohio State University at night. I was being considered for promotion into sales management, which would have been the next step. We had a marketing staff that had very little sales background, very little customer understanding. The sales manager thought I might be interested in moving into marketing to bring a sales perspective to that area.

"I stayed there for another five years. I started in marketing as an assistant product manager and left as product manager.

"Then I came to Hill-Rom as marketing manager in 1995. The move was prompted by my concern for a failing market in surgical products and the entire acute care business. Hill-Rom was following the health care market to where it was going, into long-term care and home care. I liked being in health care marketing, but I needed to follow the patient, and Kimberly-Clark wasn't showing signs that they were going to do that as part of their long-term plans. Hill-Rom approached me through a headhunter."

Expert Advice

"The best marketers have a dual background. They have been salespeople and they also have the formal education–they have an M.B.A. My preference is to get an M.B.A. the way I did. After you've been in sales for a while, then go back and get it."

(For more information about other careers in medical sales, turn to Chapter 4.)

INTERVIEW

Ernie Stetenfeld
Public Relations Director

Ernie Stetenfeld has been with AAA Wisconsin since 1987. He started in a general capacity, then worked his way up to his current position as public relations director. He earned his master's degree in journalism and mass communications at Drake University in Des Moines, Iowa in 1982.

What the Job's Really Like

"I have five major areas of purview: member relations, which is mostly a complaint-solving activity; general public relations, including news bureau activity and media relations; traffic safety promotion, which has been a AAA interest from our founding in 1902; member magazine production–until about a year ago I was editor, now I'm executive editor; and government relations and lobbying.

"I have three professional-level staff people–one who serves as an editor, one who serves primarily as public relations and media relations manager, and another who is member relations manager. There are two-and-a-half support staff people and, working for the member relations manager–we have a club of about half a million members–are six full-time employees and three part-time people.

"In the member relations area we have direct sales goals. The people who work in that area serve as the inbound telemarketing staff for AAA Wisconsin. So if a potential member calls our 800 number, for example, our staff will try to convince them that joining AAA is a good idea.

"Indirectly, and more generally, and probably more importantly, my department serves in a marketing support capacity. We're the people who garner the free publicity for AAA in Wisconsin. We serve in a media relations capacity and are out to get the good name and logo of AAA into news media across the state, a) for public information, and b) to soften the market for our marketing purposes. Our goal is to further entrench the AAA name, logo, and reputation among the general public and our member base in the state. The purpose of this is to help them to think of us in a good way when we send them some sort of marketing pitch, such as for insurance, or travel agency products or other membership products.

"We want to create an environment for AAA in the state that disposes the general public and members to think well of us in terms of reputation and as a result of that to be receptive to our attempts to market product and services.

"In a typical day I might talk to one or two members; give a few media interviews, although I give only about 30 percent of the interviews–the media relations manager does more; I might write a piece of testimony for public policy purposes. For instance, to influence legislation on the state level. I might help to edit a magazine article or write a short article for our bimonthly member publication. But I would spend probably most of my time in meetings with other department heads, trying to coordinate the activities of our various business units and do any necessary troubleshooting. In fact, today, which is a rather atypical day, 90 percent of my time has been spent troubleshooting. We recently have undergone a merger–AAA Wisconsin and AAA Michigan have joined forces–and so there are a number of things, system changes, for example, that necessitate more of my time being spent on troubleshooting than might normally be the case.

If something is related to an AAA stance on public policy and we get a question about it and need to make an announcement about it, that would tend to be in my area as well.

"I don't normally think of my job as more promotion than public relations, but there is a definite promotion component to it.

"I've always enjoyed magazine and publications work and I like editing, and that is the area I probably enjoy most. I also enjoy doing interviews, particularly for radio.

"The government relations aspect of my work probably is what I enjoy the least. Sometimes the intricacies of government relations are so arcane or convoluted and that can lead to a sense of frustration. On both the state and federal level AAA does, to some extent on selected issues, try to influence public policy, especially as it relates to motorists or other travelers. For example, we recently testified before a state senate committee in favor of legislation that would outlaw children under 16 riding in truck beds. We've had some deaths as a result of that sort of thing and that's the kind of issue AAA would back from a safety concern standpoint. I also work to track and occasionally provide AAA's input on major transportation policy in the state or even at the federal level. For instance, our state transportation budget, which spent almost all of 1995 getting passed.

"Salary-wise I started out at $24,000 and now earn in the high $50s. My job tends to be Monday through Friday with six or seven weekends throughout the year that I either travel or work here or at home. I probably work an average of 55 hours a week–it used to be longer. I was able to add another position in my department so that has freed me up significantly."

How Ernie Stetenfeld Got Started

"I got into this by virtue of having garnered some expertise in the magazine end of the spectrum. My undergraduate degree is in religion and anthropology, from Northwestern in 1979. My graduate degree is in journalism and mass comm with two emphases. One was news editorial and the other was magazine journalism. My first job was as a newspaper reporter and then shortly after I started up a trade journal in Chicago for the multi-housing industry. I enjoy magazine work and I was hired initially at AAA because of that experience I had. I had also done other forms of public relations and government relations in the interim as well."

Expert Advice

"In a PR type of job don't expect to end up just doing one thing in most instances. You'll be called on to relate to any number of different publics and to use any number of different communications tools, so it's best to broaden your arsenal."

• • •

FOR MORE INFORMATION

For information about careers in sales and marketing management, contact:

American Marketing Association
250 S. Wacker Dr.
Chicago, IL 60606

Sales and Marketing Executives International
458 Statler Office Tower
Cleveland, OH 44115

For information about careers in advertising management, contact:

American Advertising Federation Education Services
  Department
1101 Vermont Ave. NW, Suite 500
Washington, DC 20005

Information about careers in promotion management is available from:

Council of Sales Promotion Agencies
750 Summer St.
Stamford, CT 06901

Promotion Marketing Association of America, Inc.
322 Eighth Ave., Suite 1201
New York, NY 10001

Information about careers in public relations management is available from:

Public Relations Society of America
33 Irving Place
New York, NY 10003-2376

VGM CAREER BOOKS

BUSINESS PORTRAITS
Boeing
Coca-Cola
Ford
McDonald's

CAREER DIRECTORIES
Careers Encyclopedia
Dictionary of Occupational Titles
Occupational Outlook Handbook

CAREERS FOR
Animal Lovers; Bookworms; Caring
People; Computer Buffs; Crafty
People; Culture Lovers;
Environmental Types; Fashion Plates;
Film Buffs; Foreign Language
Aficionados; Good Samaritans;
Gourmets; Health Nuts; History
Buffs; Kids at Heart; Music Lovers;
Mystery Buffs; Nature Lovers; Night
Owls; Number Crunchers; Plant
Lovers; Shutterbugs; Sports Nuts;
Travel Buffs; Writers

CAREERS IN
Accounting; Advertising; Business;
Child Care; Communications;
Computers; Education; Engineering;
the Environment; Finance;
Government; Health Care; High
Tech; Horticulture & Botany;
International Business; Journalism;
Law; Marketing; Medicine; Science;
Social & Rehabilitation Services

CAREER PLANNING
Beating Job Burnout
Beginning Entrepreneur
Big Book of Jobs
Career Planning & Development for
College Students &
Recent Graduates
Career Change
Career Success for People with
Physical Disabilities
Careers Checklists
College and Career Success for Students
with Learning Disabilities
Complete Guide to Career Etiquette
Cover Letters They Don't Forget
Dr. Job's Complete Career Guide
Executive Job Search Strategies
Guide to Basic Cover Letter Writing
Guide to Basic Résumé Writing
Guide to Internet Job Searching
Guide to Temporary Employment
Job Interviewing for College Students
Joyce Lain Kennedy's Career Book

Out of Uniform
Parent's Crash Course in Career
Planning
Slame Dunk Résumés
Up Your Grades: Proven Strategies
for Academic Success

CAREER PORTRAITS
Animals; Cars; Computers;
Electronics; Fashion; Firefighting;
Music; Nature; Nursing; Science;
Sports; Teaching; Travel; Writing

GREAT JOBS FOR
Business Majors
Communications Majors
Engineering Majors
English Majors
Foreign Language Majors
History Majors
Psychology Majors
Sociology Majors

HOW TO
Apply to American Colleges and
Universities
Approach an Advertising Agency and
Walk Away with the Job You Want
Be a Super Sitter
Bounce Back Quickly After
Losing Your Job
Change Your Career
Choose the Right Career
Cómo escribir un currículum vitae en
inglés que tenga éxito
Find Your New Career Upon
Retirement
Get & Keep Your First Job
Get Hired Today
Get into the Right Business School
Get into the Right Law School
Get into the Right Medical School
Get People to Do Things Your Way
Have a Winning Job Interview
Hit the Ground Running in Your
New Job
Hold It All Together When You've
Lost Your Job
Improve Your Study Skills
Jumpstart a Stalled Career
Land a Better Job
Launch Your Career in TV News
Make the Right Career Moves
Market Your College Degree
Move from College into a
Secure Job
Negotiate the Raise You Deserve
Prepare Your Curriculum Vitae

Prepare for College
Run Your Own Home Business
Succeed in Advertising When all You
Succeed in College
Succeed in High School
Take Charge of Your Child's Early
Education
Write a Winning Résumé
Write Successful Cover Letters
Write Term Papers & Reports
Write Your College Application Essay

MADE EASY
College Applications
Cover Letters
Getting a Raise
Job Hunting
Job Interviews
Résumés

**ON THE JOB: REAL PEOPLE
WORKING IN...**
Communications
Health Care
Sales & Marketing
Service Businesses

OPPORTUNITIES IN
This extensive series provides detailed
information on more than 150
individual career fields.

RÉSUMÉS FOR
Advertising Careers
Architecture and Related Careers
Banking and Financial Careers
Business Management Careers
College Students &
Recent Graduates
Communications Careers
Computer Careers
Education Careers
Engineering Careers
Environmental Careers
Ex-Military Personnel
50+ Job Hunters
Government Careers
Health and Medical Careers
High School Graduates
High Tech Careers
Law Careers
Midcareer Job Changes
Nursing Careers
Re-Entering the Job Market
Sales and Marketing Careers
Scientific and Technical Careers
Social Service Careers
The First-Time Job Hunter

 VGM Career Horizons
a division of *NTC Publishing Group*
4255 West Touhy Avenue
Lincolnwood, Illinois 60646–1975